THE
NEW CART
CHURCH

Doing the Right Thing the Wrong Way

Jerry Scheidbach

Copyright © 2014 by Jerry Scheidbach

The New Cart Church: *Doing the Right Thing, the Wrong Way!*

Jerry Scheidbach

Printed in the United States of America

ISBN: 9780982211038

All Bible quotations are taken from the Authorized King James Bible (KJB)

Proofreading: Cassy Benefield, Barbara Melander, Becky Scheidbach, Pastor Max Graves, Zachary Scheidbach

Peer Reviewed by Dr. Benny Beckum, Pastor Jerry Cook, Pastor Larry Cox, Pastor Max Graves, Pastor Greg Kern, Evangelist Dave McCracken, Dr. Mark Rasmussen, Pastor Marshal Stevens, and Dr. Mike Sullivant.

Cover Design: Nakia Jones

The author, Jerry Scheidbach, pastors the Lighthouse Baptist Church in Santa Maria, California. He is the executive editor for *The Intercessor* magazine, and hosts *The Brain Massage®* radio show. To contact Pastor Scheidbach write to Lighthouse Baptist Church, PO Box 2803, Santa Maria, CA 93457, or call (805) 347-9887. To contact him by email use the email address DistinctivelyBaptistPub@gmail.com, or visit our websites at www.santamarialighthouse.org or www.thebrainmassageshow.com. For more books by Pastor Scheidbach, go to www.booksatdbp.com.

To Order More Copies

Go to www.booksatdbp.com

$16.55 retail; $15.00 each for 5 or more copies / $10.00 each for 10 or more copies / and $6.00 each for 50 or more copies. (For larger orders, call 805.714.0785). All prices subject to shipping & handling.

Table of Contents

Prologue

America the Religious

WHY DO SO MANY say America is on her way to hell (Psalm 9:17) when she has never known a time in her history when there were more or larger churches than she may boast of today?

Consider a few examples: *Lakewood Church,* Houston, TX, Joel Osteen, attendance, 43,500; *North Point Community Church,* Atlanta, GA, Andy Stanley, attendance, 27,429; *LifeChurch.tv,* Edmond, OK, Craig Groeschel, attendance, 26,776; *Willow Creek Community Church,* South Barrington, IL, Bill Hybels, attendance, 24,377; *Without Walls International,* Tampa, FL, Paula White, attendance, 23,900; *Southeast Christian Church,* Louisville, KY, Dave Stone, attendance, 20,801; *Saddleback Church,* Lake Forest, CA, Rick Warren, attendance 20,000+, and the list goes on for a total of 70 *gigachurches* (churches with average attendance above 10,000).[1] While the average attendance of the 330,000[2] churches

---

1 *Top 70 Largest Gigachurches in America (2011 Edition)* http://churhrelevance. com/top-71-largest-gigachurches-in-america-2011-edition/ (12/12/2012)
2 *7 Startling Facts: An Up Close Look at Church Attendance in America,* www. churchleaders.com (12/12/2012)

in America is only 75, there are almost 1,600 *megachurches* with average attendance above 2,000. California boasts the greatest number of megachurches with 178, followed by Texas with 157.[3] Of course, there have been large congregations in the past. Charles Spurgeon ministered to 6,000 in weekly attendance, and Moody Church, of Chicago, had the distinction of housing above 10,000 in its heyday under the famous evangelist. But these were exceptional, with only about 13 such churches from 1784 through 1899.

Although America may boast an unprecedented number of gigachurches and megachurches, as a percentage of population, church attendance has fallen off dramatically when compared to the great revival periods of the mid 1700s and 1800s. Nevertheless, 72% of Americans self-identify as *Christian*. Even if you narrow the sample to include only those who self-identify as born-again Christians, the number is an impressive 41%.[4] That means 41% of Americans believe that Jesus Christ is Lord, that He died for their sins, and arose from the dead the third day, and virtually all of these would say they believe the Bible is the basis for their beliefs.

Three hundred and thirty thousand churches, at least 70 gigachurches and almost 1,600 megachurches, with 72% of the population self-identifying as Christian, yet it is generally conceded that America is in moral decline.

America in Moral Decline

Conservatives ask, how can abortion continue to be legal and gay rights activists continue to gain ground in our culture when 72% of our population self-identify as Christian? Why is there not a tsunami of popular revolt against California Governor Brown and the state legislators who passed a law requiring schools to allow children from Kindergarten through 12th grade to decide their own gender

---

3 Bogan, Jesse, *America's Biggest Megachurches*, Forbes.com www.forbes. com/2009/06/26/americas-biggest-megachurches-business-megachurch/ (12/12/2012)
4 CP U.S., http://www.christianpost.com/news/study-born-53454/ Quoting a Barna report (printed 12/18/2012)

and to use whatever restroom or dressing room they choose?[5] One would expect that if Christians were so strong a majority then they would have greater influence on our nation's lawmakers.

Not all Christians agree about what constitutes morality. For example, about 41% of those who call themselves Christian believe that to oppose gay marriage or to deny reproductive rights (abortion) is immoral, even unchristian. Rejecting homosexual marriage is associated with bigotry. Denying reproductive rights is seen as insensitive to the needs of women with unwanted pregnancies. Such lack of sympathy is considered unchristian. Additionally, they view pro-life and pro-family Christians as forcing their own private morality onto others, a violation of freedom of religion and liberty of conscience. Many go so far as to equate pro-life and pro-family positions with hatred, which violates anyone's idea of what it means to be Christian. Often, Bible-believing, born-again Christians are shocked to discover that about 1 in 5 of their fellow born-again Christians believes that supporting reproductive rights and gay marriage is consistent with their Christian faith. This disparity on the subject of morality makes it necessary for me to clarify what I mean when I say that America is in moral decline.

Defining Morality The word *morality* refers to the core beliefs by which we judge a behavior as right or wrong. In America, the source of authority for our traditionally held core beliefs was the Bible. Today, almost a quarter of the American population rejects Christianity, and about half of those who call themselves Christians no longer regard the Bible as the absolute authoritative source for their beliefs. Therefore, Americans no longer share a common set of core values, or beliefs, hence we no longer have general agreement about *morality*.

Defining morality is a problem when there is no commonly agreed to authority supporting a commonly held set of values and beliefs. Today we have competing belief systems. Many have rejected

---

5 California Assembly Bill 1266, CBSNEWS http://www.cbsnews.com/8301-250_162-57598231/california-law-allows-transgender-students-to-pick-bathrooms-sports-teams-they-identify-with/ (9/3/13)

traditional American values and beliefs, while many others are questioning them, and still others are confused and don't know what to believe. At the same time, there is a significant, though shrinking, number of conservative, born-again Christians who continue to hold to the core beliefs founded upon the Bible and the morality that is shaped by those beliefs.

Defining Moral Decline If succeeding generations adopt moral views that are contrary to those of the prior generation, it will create division and conflict in the social structure. In our culture, those holding to the traditional moral viewpoint are called *traditionalists*. Those advocating a new morality are called *progressives*. On one hand, traditionalists will inevitably regard the new morality to be a decline from the true or right moral position. On the other hand, the progressives will energetically argue that the old morality is out of date and enthusiastically embrace the new morality as enlightened, even liberating. America is in an argument with her past.

Ironically, although Americans are deeply divided over the meaning of morality, virtually all Americans believe America is in moral decline. Traditionalist and progressive Christians agree that the deterioration of the family, the rise in suicide among our youth, and the increase of violence in our culture are a few of the many signs of moral decline. However, traditionalists see a relationship between the values and beliefs that legitimize murdering babies in the womb and that distort the divine design of marriage with the problems we all agree signal trouble for the future of our country. Progressives disagree.

I am a traditionalist Christian. I believe that the moral decline in America is the result of Americans turning their backs on the teachings of the Bible. I ask my progressive, born-again Christian friends to answer a simple question. Are our children safer today than they were when the overwhelming majority of America's Christians held to the Bible as the final authority for matters of morality?

One example: when shared cultural views of sexuality were based on the teachings of the Bible did we have three million teens contracting a sexually transmitted disease each year?

OK, two examples: when the biblical model shaped our cultural views of the family did we have a 50% divorce rate?

When the Bible was our guide, do you think you ever would have read that, "Political leaders were afraid to say married families were better for children than cohabiting families or single parent families"?[6] Isn't it obvious that the biblical model of the family is better for children? Politicians today, however, are afraid to admit it, even when confronted with scientific studies that confirm it. The relationship between the breakdown of family and the rise in gang violence is well documented. And the relationship between promiscuity and the breakdown of the family is also well documented. These things are related. If we leave the teaching of the Bible on morality in one area, it necessarily results in a breakdown in morality in other areas also.

Churches of born-again Christians who accept the Bible as the basis for their beliefs are key to restoring America to her traditional values and morals that are rooted in the Bible. Yet these born-again Christians are divided between traditionalist believers whose moral sense is shaped by a traditional understanding of Scripture, and progressive believers whose moral views are not.

Sadly, many who accept the Bible as their authority for faith and life have surrendered to progressive ideas. Some have done so because they have been betrayed by their spiritual leaders and so don't know better. Others do so in order to avoid conflict with the world, or to avoid being marginalized in society. In either case, many of these Christians see themselves as conservatives. Almost weekly, I talk to some among my fellow Americans who say they are conservative but whose opinions on important social issues are progressive. This is true not only among those who distinguish between social and fiscal issues. I find there are many who think they are social and fiscal conservatives whose views on important moral questions do not square with traditional Christian views.

---

6 http://www.dailymail.co.uk/news/article-2279326/Decline-marriage-children-growing-fathers-doing-harm-smoking-global-warming-poor-diets-says-Baroness.html#ixzz2LNrt1NFQ (2/19/13)

Still there are others who call themselves conservative and whose opinions square up with that profession who nevertheless are *progressive* in their methods of evangelism and church identification. They support compromising churches that provide very little, if any, *salt* or *light* influence in their respective communities (Matthew 5:13-14). Instead, they support churches that go out of their way to avoid doing what Jesus specifically sent the Spirit into the world to do: to "reprove the world of sin, and of righteousness, and of judgment" (John 16:7-13). When conservative Christians support and identify with liberal congregations they stand as a roadblock to restoring America to her traditional values rooted in biblical Christianity.

In this book, I explain why I use the expression *new cart* to identify progressive churches and the Christians who support them. Furthermore, I show that God places the blame for the moral decline in America at the feet of new cart pastors who have sought the favor of the people and have not sought the LORD,[7] along with the people who "love to have it so" (Jeremiah 5:31; 10:21). I shall show that the answer to restoring America to her moral roots, and thus avert divine judgment, is the same answer God gave Judah when He called them to ask for the "old paths" and to walk therein (Jeremiah 6:16). It is my sincere hope that Christ, the Chief Shepherd, will use this book to speak to the hearts of His sheep and call them out of the new cart church and into an old path church, before it is too late. Because America is heading for judgment, and "judgment must begin at the house of God" (I Peter 4:17; I Timothy 3:15).

---

7 In the King James Bible, the word *lord* written with capital L followed by small caps LORD indicates that it is a translation of the Hebrew word for the Name of God, or *Jehovah*. When rendered with capital L and lower case letters, as in Lord, it translates the Hebrew word *adoni*. I follow the form used in the King James Bible.

Chapter One

A New Cart

King David and his new cart: *a good man, doing a good thing, the wrong way!*

DAVID WAS A GOOD man who wanted to do the right thing. But when he tried to do the right thing the wrong way, he brought death into the congregation of the LORD.

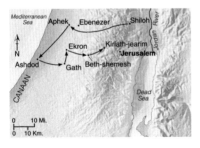

For over 68 years, the Ark of the Covenant had been separated from the Tabernacle where it belonged, and for most of that time it was kept in a border city between Judah and Benjamin.[8] When David became king, God stirred in his heart a desire to bring the Ark to Mount Zion in Jerusalem.

---

8 According to I Samuel 6:1, the Ark had been with the Philistines for seven months. I Samuel 7:2 informs us it was in the house of Abinadab for 20 years. David brought the Ark to Jerusalem after the end of Saul's reign, and Saul reigned for 40 years (Acts 13:21). David was anointed king of Judah about four days after Saul's death (II Samuel 1:1-4. He reigned in Hebron seven years and six months before he was anointed king of all Israel (II Samuel 5:5). After Uzzah died for touching the Ark, David left it in the house of Obed-Edom for three months (II Samuel 6:11). Therefore, the Ark was not returned to the Tabernacle for at least 68 years, four months, and four days.

David had a new cart built to carry the Ark, but this proved to be a disaster. One man was killed, and the plan to bring the Ark to Jerusalem fell apart. It was the right thing to do, but it was the wrong way to do it. To appreciate the significance of this story to the point of this book, we will take a moment to explain what is this Ark, why it was important to the Israelites, why it had been taken out of the Tabernacle, and why David's chosen method for obeying God's will failed.

Moses was instructed to build a throne for God on earth (Exodus 25). Constructed as a chest from acacia wood and overlaid with gold, the throne was to contain the precious tables of stone upon which God wrote His Law, some of the manna with which He fed Israel in the wilderness, and the rod of Aaron that budded supernaturally as a witness that Aaron and his seed alone were to serve as God's high priest. Over the top of the chest, Moses was instructed to place the mercy seat, which was made of pure gold (Exodus 25:17).

This golden covered box with the pure gold mercy seat was called the *Ark of the Covenant* because it contained the agreement that God made with Israel and represented God's presence with His people.

The Ark was kept in the Tabernacle behind a very thick veil and only the high priest, once each year, was allowed to approach it. The most important piece of furniture in the Tabernacle, the Ark represented the place on earth where God would dwell with His people (Exodus 30:6). Moses was given very clear instructions on how the Ark was to be carried (Exodus 25-26).

After Joshua led Israel into Canaan, in the days before Israel had a king, the Tabernacle was set up in Shiloh, about 20 miles north of Jerusalem. The Ark remained with the Tabernacle until the end of the priesthood of Eli (I Samuel 1-5). His sons were vile and wicked, and he failed to restrain them. Under their leadership the people drifted away from the LORD. War broke out between Israel and the neighboring Philistines.[9] The Philistines were winning.

Israel's leaders thought they could win against the Philistines if they followed the Ark into battle. They carried it out of the Tabernacle to their camp in a city called Ebenezer. The Philistines were encamped at nearby Aphek.

God did not honor the Israelites' superstition about the Ark. The Philistines overcame them and captured the Ark of the Covenant. They killed Eli's wicked sons, and carried the Ark from Ebenezer to their capital city, Ashdod. When word of this reached Eli, he fell from his seat, broke his neck, and died. The wife of one of Eli's sons was pregnant at the time and went into premature labor when she

heard the Ark was lost. She named her son *Ichabod*, which means *the glory is departed.* Then she died. Meanwhile, the Philistines placed the Ark in a temple of their god, Dagon (I Samuel 5).

In the morning, the priests of the Philistines entered into their temple and found their idol of Dagon fallen from its pedestal on its face before the Ark of the LORD (I Samuel 5:3). They picked up their god and replaced it on its pedestal. The next morning, when the priests returned to the temple of Dagon, they found their idol again prostrate before the Ark of the LORD, but this time the head and both the palms of its hands were cut off and were set upon the threshold of its pedestal. "Only the stump of Dagon was left to him" (I Samuel 5:4). The pagan priests were perplexed and vexed.

God chastised the people of Ashdod. They were covered with painful boils, and their homes were overrun with mice (I Samuel 6:5). When the plague spread to the coasts of Ashdod (I Samuel 5:6-7), the city's leaders decided to send the Ark of God to another Philistine city called Gath (I Samuel 5:8). But the plague of the boils

---

9 The word *Philistine* corresponds to the modern day term *Palestinian,* and refers to the anti-Semitic people of the land once called Canaan.

and mice only worsened so they sent the Ark to yet another Philistine city called Ekron (I Samuel 5:10). The Ekronites wanted nothing to do with this Ark of God and they refused to keep it (I Samuel 5:11). The chief leaders of the Philistines consulted together and counseled the people to send the Ark out of Philistia.

After seven months of the plague of the boils and the mice (I Samuel 6:1), the Ark of God was placed on a new cart that was drawn by two milk cows. The Philistines watched to see which way the cows would take the Ark. They reasoned that if the cows carried the Ark back to Israel, then the plague of the boils and the mice was indeed a judgment from the God of Israel (I Samuel 6:9). The Philistines followed the cart until it crossed into a city of Israel called Bethshemesh.

The men of Bethshemesh offended the LORD because they opened the Ark and looked inside (I Samuel 6:19). Moses gave specific instructions prohibiting any but the house of Levi to approach the Ark (Deuteronomy 10:8). Philistines ignorant of Moses' Law showed more reverence toward the Ark than did these men of Israel. Over 50,000 died in Bethshemesh for this offense (I Samuel 6:19). In fear and trembling, they sent messengers to Kirjathjearim, the border city between Benjamin and Judah, and asked them to take the Ark out of their city. The Ark was then taken into Kirjathjearim, and kept in the house of Abinadab (I Samuel 7:2).

After Saul died (II Samuel 1:1), and David was anointed king over all Israel (II Samuel 5:1-5), God stirred his heart to move the Ark to Mount Zion in Jerusalem. The leadership and all the people encouraged him in his purpose (I Chronicles 13:1-4). David was a man after God's own heart (I Samuel 13:14; Acts 13:22). He was a good man (Psalm 37:23; Matthew 12:35). What he wanted to do was a good thing; indeed, it was the will of God.

But David did not inquire of the LORD how to transport the Ark. Instead, he chose the method of the Philistines, and commissioned the construction of a new cart to carry it to Jerusalem (I Samuel 6:7; II Samuel 6:3; I Chronicles 13:7). This was a grave error.

All Israel gathered at the home of Abinadab (II Samuel 6:3; I Chronicles 13:7). The Ark was placed on the new cart that David had commissioned especially for the purpose. The two sons of Abinadab, Uzzah and Ahio, were given the honor of driving the cart. Ahio led the oxen while Uzzah held the reins and sat in the cart with the Ark. The oxen stumbled, the Ark rocked, and Uzzah reached his hand back to steady it (II Samuel 6:6; I Chronicles 13:9). The moment he touched the Ark God's wrath was kindled and He smote Uzzah. And there he died (I Chronicles 13:10).

David was shocked that God would do this. After all, David was doing what God wanted him to do. It was a good thing, and it was the will of God. Why would God send death into the camp on such a glorious occasion? David was grieved. He was afraid of God and decided not to bring the Ark to Jerusalem (II Samuel 6:9). Instead, he took it aside to the house of a Levite named Obededom (II Samuel 6:10). It remained there for three months (I Chronicles 13:12-14).

Obededom was blessed! It soon became clear to everyone that the blessing of God was with the Ark.

Perhaps one of the prophets, or a Levite, brought to David's attention the passage in the Law of Moses that laid out God's express instructions for how the Ark was to be handled. Maybe he came across it as he worked on writing out a copy of the Law of Moses (Deuteronomy 17:18). Somehow he learned that God strictly prohibited the Ark to be approached by any but the Levites, and that God had given very specific instructions regarding how it was to be transported (I Chronicles 15:2). David learned what he had done wrong. He informed the congregation that only the Levites were to move the Ark, and that it had to be done according to the Scriptures.

David decided they would try again to bring the Ark to Jerusalem (I Chronicles 15). He organized the congregation to move it according to the directions given in the Scriptures. The Ark was triumphantly, and safely, moved to Mount Zion and pitched in the tent David prepared for it (II Samuel 6:17). Finally, the Ark of God was placed in God's chosen city with His chosen people by His chosen servant.

David was a good man, and he wanted to do a good thing. However, he went about doing it in the wrong way. He chose to use the method of the Philistines—a new cart. It worked well for the Philistines, but God did not honor this method when used by David. Even though David was a good man, doing a good thing, and doing the will of God, his effort was not blessed because he failed to do it God's way.

The moral of this story is that it's not enough to have good motives and to be doing something you know that God told you to do; it's important also that you obey God in the way you do it.

Many good men are laboring sincerely to do the good work of evangelism, which is certainly something God has commanded us to do, but they are not doing it God's way. They are using the methods of the Philistines. That might work well for the Philistines, but it will never work for God's people. It has brought death into the churches. Indeed, it is because so many are using the world's ways to do the work of God that many churches have a name that they are alive, but they are dead (Revelation 3:1).

Jesus said, "I will build my church" (Matthew 16:18). It's one thing to build a large crowd. Anyone with charisma, lots of money, and a willingness to tickle ears or to appeal to the fleshly appetites of worldly Christians can build a large crowd. But only Jesus can build a church.

There are several gigachurches and almost 2,000 megachurches, but most of these were built using the methods of the *Philistines*— that is, worldly methods. These are new cart churches. For the most part, these churches were built by well-meaning men who desired to do a good thing. Unfortunately, they decided to follow the way of the world in their methods.

Like the ancient church at Sardis, these new cart churches have a name that they live, and indeed appear to be very much alive; but in truth they are dead (Revelation 3:1). And they export this spiritual death into the churches that follow them. That is why we have the paradox of more large churches than ever before with an ever-shrinking percentage of the population attending any church.

The problems created by new cart Christianity go well beyond church attendance. It is also the reason this nation is in a moral free fall into corruption despite roughly 72% of the American population claiming to be Christian. It affects us economically, politically, and culturally. It is the reason this nation is forgetting God, and it is the root cause why this nation under God is about to be turned into hell (Psalm 9:17).

Unless new cart Christians wake up and return to the old paths, America will lose her place in the earth as one nation under God with liberty and justice for all.

Chapter Two

The Old Paths

"Thus saith the LORD, stand ye in the ways, and see, and ask for the old paths, where is the good way, and walk therein, and ye shall find rest for your souls" (Jeremiah 6:16).

HOW DOES SOMETHING SAID by an Old Testament prophet to God's people 2,600 years ago relate to God's people in America today? I intend to show that, according to the Bible, what was said by Jeremiah to Judah back then was specifically intended for us today! And it is especially applicable to America.

Judah had offended God. Judgment was imminent. Yet God offered to them an opportunity to avert their judgment. His counsel to them was to walk in the old paths. Obviously, Judah had gotten off the paths of righteousness and strayed away from the LORD onto new paths that led them into sins that provoked God to wrath. To avoid judgment they needed to return to the LORD. To return to the LORD they needed to return to the old ways, the old paths.

Like Judah, America has strayed away from the old paths that led her to become "one nation under God." To forestall judgment, the answer is the same: America needs to return to the old paths. But isn't the parallel between Judah and America a mere coincidence? Can we say the prophecy of Jeremiah was intended by God to be His message to America today?

Some seducing spirit, desiring to neutralize the impact of God's Word upon our conscience, will say, "Well, that was written a long time ago to Judah and is not relevant to us today." Consider the following four reasons we should understand Jeremiah's words as directed particularly to Christians today with a specific application to America.

First, according to the Bible, what was written nearly 2,600 years ago by Jeremiah to God's people is actually more relevant to believers today than it was to the believers in his day. Does that surprise you?

According to Paul, all Scripture is profitable to us today (II Timothy 3:16). Speaking specifically of what was written in the Old Testament, the Apostle Paul declared, "Now all these things happened unto them for ensamples: and they are written for our admonition, upon whom the ends of the world are come" (I Corinthians 10:11). In the book of Romans Paul, by the Spirit, wrote, "For whatsoever things were written aforetime were written for our learning, that we through patience and comfort of the scriptures might have hope" (Romans 15:4). According to the Bible, God had us primarily in view when He inspired the writers of the Old Testament.

I'm not saying we carry forward the ordinances of the Law (Colossians 2:16-23); nevertheless, even those rituals are instructive as examples and illustrations of truths that we find clarified in the New Testament. But my point is that I Corinthians 10:11 and Romans 15:4 say that God providentially intervened in the history of His people and did things back then that He intended would be recorded in Scripture for us upon whom the ends of the world are come. And Paul says that means you and me. We live in the last days, and we are the people upon whom the ends of the world are come (Hebrews 1:2; Acts 2:17; II Peter 3:3).

Obviously, what was revealed by God to the prophets of the Old Testament served their generation. But according to the Bible, what God did and what He had written down was specifically for us upon whom the ends of the world are come. Clearly, the Old Testament was written very specifically for us.

Second, Judah and America were each raised up by God to be a nation identified as peculiarly His among the nations of the earth. God exalted these nations, giving to them the kingdom.

God's kingdom presides over the kingdoms of the world, and He raises up whatever nation He chooses to serve as His steward of the kingdom (Daniel 4:17, 25, 32)! Nations appointed to this honor are exalted above all other nations of the earth.

By the time Jesus came into the world Satan had been given all earthly kingdoms along with the power to appoint over them whomever he would (Matthew 4:8-9; Luke 4:5-6). But God sent His own Son, Jesus Christ, Who spoiled the house of Satan, and all power (authority) in Heaven and in earth was transferred to our LORD (Matthew 28:18; Colossians 2:14-15). Today, the ruler of all of Heaven and earth is the Son of God, Jesus Christ (Matthew 28:18).

Jesus left the keys of the kingdom to His church (Matthew 16:18). He promised that whatever nation brought forth the fruit of the kingdom would receive Heaven's favored nation status (Matthew 21:43).

"Blessed is the nation whose God is the LORD; and the people whom He hath chosen for His own inheritance" (Psalm 33:12) applies very specifically to that "chosen generation, a royal priesthood, an holy nation, a peculiar people…" spoken of by the Spirit through the Apostle Peter (I Peter 2:9-10). And by extension, it applies to the nation that receives them and their message (Matthew 10:13; Luke 10:5).[10]

Therefore, if a nation receives the gospel preached by the true church, the keys of the kingdom are employed to open the doors of the kingdom to that people and Heaven's blessings favor that nation. So long as such a nation acknowledges the LORDSHIP of Jesus Christ, and honors Him, it will receive His blessing and favor.

---

10 These verses speak of us granting the blessing of our peace upon a house that receives us and our message. We know it can be extended to apply to cities (Matthew 10:14; Luke 9:5). Because we are commanded to teach all *nations* (Matthew 28:19), it is reasonable to extend the application to nations as well.

Patrick Henry observed that America was founded upon the gospel of Jesus Christ, and our history confirms this to be true. From the notes of James Madison, on June 28, 1787, while Congress argued over how to frame our Constitution, we learn that Benjamin Franklin called on the Congress to pray for wisdom. Among other things he said to implore the founders to prayer is this famous quote: "I have lived, sir, a long time, and the longer I live the more convincing proofs I see of this truth—that God governs in the affairs of men. And if a sparrow cannot fall to the ground without His notice, is it probable that an empire can rise without His aid?"[11] But a greater authority than Benjamin Franklin affirms what that Founder learned from observation. As we have seen, Daniel the prophet plainly tells us that God raises nations, and nothing else can explain the phenomenon of America's rise to world domination.

During the time of her kingdom, Judah was the nation under God that enjoyed Heaven's peculiar blessing and favor among the nations of the earth. America is that nation today. Judah turned away from God and was brought into disfavor with Him and finally to destruction. America has likewise turned from God and now faces the promise of His divine wrath. "Be not deceived; God is not mocked: for whatsoever a man soweth, that shall he also reap" certainly applies to nations as well as to persons (Galatians 6:9).

Third, when we compare the sins of Judah that provoked God to destroy her among the nations it is impossible to miss the parallels with our own nation.

Judah proved to be unfaithful in her stewardship of the kingdom. She was reduced in glory and made a byword of shame to the world so that she sang, "Thou makest us a byword among the heathen, a shaking of the head among the people" (Psalm 44:14). America has been unfaithful to the God of nations. America will lose her glory and become the mock of fools.

Anyone reading God's indictment declared against Judah through Jeremiah will readily see that America is equally culpable: we have

---

11 http://candst.tripod.com/franklin.htm (2/15/14)

forgotten God (Jeremiah 2:32); our culture is overrun with stealing, murder, adultery, and idolatry (Jeremiah 7:9); we have exalted the wicked (Jeremiah 8:1-2; Proverbs 28:4); we have corrupted judgment (Jeremiah 5:1; Isaiah 59:14); we have chosen death (Jeremiah 8:3; 9:21); and we wholly are given over to whoredoms (Jeremiah 5:8; Hebrews 13:4).

Most believers would probably agree that America is heading straight into the fist of God. Harbingers of judgment are everywhere evident, and disastrous judgment is imminent. Most believers, however, do not understand that judgment begins in the house of God (I Peter 4:17).

Judgment begins in the house of God because the corruptions that have brought us to this place began in the house of God, the church of the living God, the pillar and ground of the truth (I Timothy 3:15).

This bring us to the fourth reason that confirms what Jeremiah said to Judah applies to America today. It is that what God reveals is the root cause of Judah's decline and fall, and it is identical to the root cause of America's decline. It is declared in Jeremiah 10:19-22 and is the topic of our next chapter.

Chapter Three

Baalism:
Then and Now

HOW DID JUDAH STRAY so far away from the old paths of her founding? The answer to that question provides insight into how America has wandered so far from hers. Moreover, we will also gain insight into something even more mysterious—how is it that so few Christians today understand their role in the decline of America? Sometimes when I'm praying I think I hear God crying:

> Woe is me for my hurt! my wound is grievous: but I said, Truly this is a grief, and I must bear it. My tabernacle is spoiled, and all my cords are broken: my children are gone forth of me, and they are not: there is none to stretch forth my tent any more, and to set up my curtains. For the pastors are become brutish, and have not sought the LORD: therefore they shall not prosper, and all their flocks shall be scattered. Behold the noise of the bruit (alarm) is come, and a great commotion out of the north country, to make the cities of Judah desolate, and a den of dragons. (Jeremiah 10:19-22)

God is speaking here! He said, "Woe is me for my hurt." What wounded Him in the days of Jeremiah is that His Tabernacle was spoiled! In other words, it was robbed of its treasures.

It's true that the wickedness of Judah provoked God to deliver them to the judgment of Nebuchadnezzar, king of Babylon (modern day Iraq), who spoiled the treasures of Solomon's Temple and carried them into Babylon (II Chronicles 36:7). However, we cannot be certain that this prophecy was given before or after Nebuchadnezzar spoiled the Temple. Establishing the chronology of Jeremiah's prophecies as recorded in his book is difficult. What we can know for certain, however, is that this prophecy is not about the Temple of Solomon. He is referring to the Tabernacle of Moses. Notice the mention of the broken cords, the tent, and the curtains (Jeremiah 10:20). Solomon's Temple was not a tent held up by cords.

Moses was given the Tabernacle as a house for God's Temple, the Holy Place, where He dwelt between the cherubim over the Mercy Seat atop the Ark of the Covenant. It was the place on earth where God would dwell with His people and manifest before them. God was wounded because His people forsook Him; they turned their hearts away from Him to other gods. He lamented that there was no one remaining in Judah who would prepare the Temple for God's presence: "There is none to stretch forth my tent any more, and to set up my curtains" (Jeremiah 10:20). They had grieved the Spirit of God so that He would not fill His Temple as before and manifest His glory in their midst.

The parallels today are troubling. The body of the believer is the Temple of God today (I Corinthians 6:19). The church is God's appointed house for His Temple (I Timothy 3:15). The New Testament believer is a priest unto God, responsible to present spiritual sacrifices (I Peter 2:5).

For example, our body is to be presented as a living sacrifice, holy, acceptable to God (Romans 12:1-2). We present the body separated from the world (holy) and dedicated to His service so that God may fill the Temple with His Spirit (Ephesians 5:18). However, believers today neglect their spiritual responsibilities, and they grieve the

Holy Spirit and quench Him (Ephesians 4:30-31; I Thessalonians 5:19). Like Judah, we have departed from the Lord following after seducing spirits that teach doctrines of devils (I Timothy 4:1-4).

There is another, yet more troubling parallel. Judah was not aware that they had departed from God, or that He had departed from them. The prophets presumed they spoke for God; the kings and princes presumed God was on their side. Jeremiah was branded a traitor because he proclaimed God would destroy the kingdom of Judah and lift up a heathen king to rule over them. This is surprising when we consider that no one claimed that Jeremiah was wrong in his assessment of the moral character of the people or the nation. Apparently, they accepted his accusations against them, but objected to the idea that God would judge them for their sins. One sin, however, they did deny. They were sensitive to at least one accusation. They denied his charge that they had gone after Baal.

The method Satan used to seduce Judah away from the old paths and blind them to their condition is the same method he has used in America—*Baalism.*

Twelve times, Jeremiah accuses Judah of having turned to the false gods of Baalim (Jeremiah 2:8, 23; 7:9; 9:14; 11:13, 17; 12:16; 19:5; 23:13, 27; 32:39, 35). Yet they denied it. The prophet was chagrined at their dullness: "How canst thou say, I am not polluted, I have not gone after Baalim?" (Jeremiah 2:23). What does it mean to go after Baalim? How could Judah have done this without being aware of it?

Many mistakenly think the word *Baal* identifies one among many pagan deities. However, Baalism identifies the religious umbrella under which many of the heathen worshiped their respective deities.

The Zidonians worshiped Ashtoreth; the Ammonites worshiped Milcom; and the Moabites worshiped Chemosh (I Kings 11:33). Yet all of these could say they worshiped *Baal.*

We know that the Moabites worshiped Chemosh (I Kings 11:33). When Israel passed through Moab, in the mountain range of *Peor,* the Bible says they turned from God to *Baalpeor* (Numbers 25:3-5; Psalm 106:28; Amos 5:26; Deuteronomy 3:29; 4:46). So, Baalpeor means the *Baal* of *Peor* (Numbers 23:28; 25:18; see Joshua 22:17).[12] The Holy Spirit, through the prophet Jeremiah, declared that the heathen never change their gods (Jeremiah 2:11). Since Peor is in Moab, and the Moabites worshiped Chemosh, we can be sure that the Baal of Peor was Chemosh (Numbers 21:29). In another example, we know that Jezebel was a priestess of Zidon and worshiped Ashtoreth, yet we are told she was promoting Baalism in Israel. Apparently, the Baal of Zidon was Ashtoreth. From this we can see that the heathen used the word *Baal* (means *the head*) as a generic term for deity.

Explaining the complex heathen concept of a plurality of gods united in a sort of corporate *deity* vying against one another for supremacy through the tribes that worshiped them goes beyond the interest of this book. Suffice it here to say that Baal was a generic term for deity among the heathen. It served as a common denominator uniting under one umbrella all pagan deities juxtaposed to the biblical notion of One, True God. It's an expression similar to the modern concept of *a supreme being*, and it's the way that many who call themselves Christian use the word *God* today!

We may justly liken Baalism to modern-day ecumenicism, where all worship of deity is considered legitimate no matter by what name the deity is called, or what forms are used to worship that deity.

How is it possible for God's own people to turn from worshiping Him to worshiping Baal, and not even know it?

Solomon was the first king to introduce idolatry into the kingdom of Israel (I Kings 11:1-4). For this sin, God divided the kingdom (I Kings 11:11-13). Judah and Benjamin together comprised the Southern kingdom that was called Judah. The other ten tribes together comprised the Northern kingdom and was called Israel.

Jezebel was a pagan priestess and the wife of Ahab, the seventh king of Israel. She introduced Baalism to God's people (I Kings 16:31) and it finally led to their destruction. A daughter of Jezebel, Athaliah, married Jehoram, the fifth king of Judah, and introduced

---

12 Keil & Delitzsch, <u>Old Testament Commentaries</u>, Vol. 1, p. 911

this corruption into that nation (II Kings 8:18-27). It finally took root and led them to destruction (II Kings 21:13).

Satan used a Jezebel to plant Baalism in the Old Testament congregation of the Lord. Eight hundred plus years later, he used another Jezebel to plant Baalism in the New Testament congregation of the Lord.

Jesus came, established His congregation (the church) and gave to her the keys of the kingdom. Satan set out to destroy the Lord's congregation, and he used the same tactic he used before—a Jezebel was planted in the church at Thyatira and she introduced Baalism to God's people (Revelation 2:20). The seeds of her false doctrines have grown into the great whore of Revelation 17. We are told that she will corrupt all nations of the earth (Revelation 17:1-2).[13]

We see the influence of Jezebel's Baalism upon believers today in the ecumenical movement, which says all faiths are essentially the same, and that we all worship God only by different names and in different ways. Because of this, I fear that most who self-identify as Christian today are like the Samaritan woman Jesus met at Jacob's well. She sincerely believed she worshiped the God of Abraham, Isaac, and Jacob, yet Jesus said to her, "Ye worship ye know not what" (John 4:22). Like the Samaritan woman there are many who profess themselves to be Christian but know not what they worship. Thus is the deceptive power of the ecumenical spirit of Baal.

We know Israel and Judah were fickle, easily seduced by the heathen who surrounded them (Ezekiel 23). No doubt it was their desire to be loved by their neighbors and to live comfortably with them that encouraged them to compromise (Jeremiah 2:33). And yet

13 The Vatican, under Pope John Paul II, on October 27, 1986, at the Basilica of St. Francis, in Assisi, Italy, hosted a worldwide ecumenical prayer meeting that included leaders from virtually every religion in the world. (See http://www.youtube.com/watch?v=w5Ke7Tn3uOU (2/8/14) at about 15 minutes into the presentation, provided by Dave Hunt ministries.) The ecumenical prayer meeting of Assisi has come to be called "the scandal of Assisi" among Catholics who object to the Pope's ecumenicism. Currently, there is a great struggle within the Roman Catholic Church over this issue. (See the Society of St. Pius X website, http://archives.sspx.org/news/assisi_iii/assisi_iii.htm (2/8/14).)

one wonders how they could have gone so far as to forget the true and living God and then to embrace the false gods of Baal.

The dilemma is largely explained when we understand that the religious idea of Baalism allowed the Israelites to worship their Baal (their Head) under the name Jehovah, and it also allowed them to keep their religious traditions. It only required them to agree that Jehovah was not the exclusive true and living God. Like the heathen who boasted their Baal was greater than that of another tribe, Israel could boast their Baal was greater. What they could not do is claim theirs was the only true God.

Furthermore, in a discussion about deity with their heathen neighbors, the Israelites could see some similarities with their own faith. By accentuating the points of seeming agreement, and deemphasizing the differences, so long as they would concede the idea of exclusivity, they could get along with their neighbors and blend in. This resulted in God's people finally adopting some of the forms of worship used by the heathen. Soon, it became impossible to distinguish between the congregation of the LORD and the congregations of their heathen neighbors. It was the ancient equivalent of modern-day ecumenicism.

Today, non-Christians and Christians alike use the word *God* in the same way the ancient heathen used the word *Baal*. Most who call themselves Christian reject the exclusivity of the gospel; they express discomfort at the absolutism of Jesus Christ Who said, "I am the way, the truth, and the life, no man cometh unto the Father but by me" (John 14:6). Many who self-identify as Christians today believe everyone worships the same God, only by different names and in different forms.

For example, many evangelical Christians believe the Mormon idea of God is equivalent to the traditional Christian view of God. This would have been dismissed as absurd only 50 years ago.

Billy Graham led most evangelical Christians to embrace the ecumenical spirit. He strayed so far from the old path that he began to deny a literal hell fire, and embrace the false gospel preached by the Roman Catholic Church.[14]

Today, some very popular evangelical ministers are closet prophets of Baalism, such as Rick Warren and Joel Osteen. I mention these two because of their wide popularity with Americans who self-identify as born-again Christians and because they both purport to be Bible-believing evangelical pastors.

Warren is pastor of Saddleback Church in California. He is a member of Tony Blair's Interfaith Advisory Council,[15] a member of the Council on Foreign Relations,[16] promotes globalism, and is neck deep in ecumenism. As noted in a 2007 article published in the *New York Times*, Rick Warren signed a document titled "A Common Word Between Us and You."[17] The document suggests Muslims and Christians worship the same God and in it there is an informal pledge not to proselytize (read, evangelize) one another. In his efforts to build bridges with Islam, he has made statements many respected Christian leaders believe amounts to saying Muslims and Christians worship the same God.[18]

---

14 When Billy Graham received an honorary doctorate from Belmont Abbey in 1967, he praised that Catholic institution's ecumenism and said, "The gospel that built this school and the gospel that brings me here tonight is still the way to salvation." Paul Smith, Gazette staff reporter, The Gastonia Gazette, Gastonia, North Carolina (11/22/1967). Regarding hell, Billy Graham's position is well known. He does not believe the fire is literal. During an interview with Richard Ostling, *Time* (11/15/1993), he said, "When it comes to hell fire I don't preach it because I'm not sure about it."

15 http://www.tonyblairfaithfoundation.org/page/who-we-are (1/30/14)

16 http://www.cfr.org/about/membership/roster.html?letter=W (1/30/14)

17 Edwards, Justin, John Piper On Rick Warren's Chrislam, http://standupforthe-truth.com/2012/02/john-piper-on-rick-warrens-chrislam/ (1/29/14), quoting the document, A Common Word Between Us and You described by King Abdullah of Jordan as "the backbone for future interfaith harmony between Islam and Christianity."

18 See http://www.beliefnet.com/News/Home-Page-News-and-Views/rick-warren-and-chrislam.aspx?p=1 (1/30/14) for what I think is a very fair and balanced exploration of this issue. Also see John Piper's statement regarding Chrislam and his concern about Rick Warren signing the statement above: http://airocross.com/2012/02/28/john-piper-on-rick-warrens-chrislam/ (1/30/14)

Warren denies that he is promulgating a new religion called Chrislam, but he has not withdrawn his signature from "A Common Word Between Us and You." Also, he continues to accept speaking engagements, for example, from the Islamic Society of North America (ISNA), which is known to be a front organization for the Muslim Brotherhood.[19]

As for Joel Osteen, one only needs to view his interview with Larry King on June 20, 2005. He equivocates, crawfishes, and slithers about attempting to avoid very simple questions regarding the doctrine of hell and the exclusivity of Jesus Christ. In one exchange, Larry King presses Osteen to say whether or not if people disagree with his gospel they will go to hell. Recounting his time in India with his father, Osteen said, "I don't know about their religion, but I know they love God."[20] Of course, Joel Osteen knows that the religion in India is predominantly Hindu. So he is essentially saying the Hindi and Christians worship the same God.

Like Warren, Osteen backs up from these sorts of statements when he is confronted by evangelicals who object. In Osteen's case, he published an open letter on his website apologizing for making that above statements. One wonders if he would return to Larry King Live and make that apology. It is doubtful. Osteen's trademark equivocating is not reserved only for when he is faced with the probing questions of a Larry King, but also when he is faced with probing questions from his fellow evangelicals. He goes out of his way to appear agreeable to whomever at the moment he is talking.

Most of Christianity today has been seduced into the ecumenical movement, today's equivalent to ancient Baalism. It has created a giant religious blender in which Christianity is being mixed together with all other religions of the world into a one-world religious puree. The Christian faith is becoming increasingly indistinguishable from other religions in the world.

---

19 Farrah, Joseph, http://www.wnd.com/2009/07/102848/ (1/30/14)

20 See http://www.youtube.com/watch?v=pKF_QgNezBY&noredirect=1 (1/30/14) to watch the video. For a copy of the transcript, see http://www.freere-public.com/focus/religion/1428853/posts (1/30/14).

God will never bless His congregation with a renewed manifestation of His glory and power under such circumstances. It would mistakenly be taken as affirmation of every false sect of Christianity, every cult using that name, as well as many other false religions. God will not openly identify Himself with worshipers of Baal.

In past revivals almost any Christian church could put out a sign calling for a prayer meeting and those gathering to pray were in sufficient agreement in essential Bible truth that God could openly identify with them and bless their prayer for revival. Today, many claim the title *Christian* who are like the Samaritan woman who knew not what she worshiped (John 4:22). Therefore, it is necessary for God to differentiate Himself from all other gods by calling His people out from among the others before He will openly declare Himself and publicly identify which congregation is His. This is what Jeremiah was telling Judah when He said they were to ask for the old paths and walk therein (Jeremiah 6:16).

In the next chapter I will show that the ultimate responsibility for Baalism taking hold in our churches and this nation is to be laid at the feet of weak, compromising pastors.

Chapter Four

The Pastors of Baal

"Woe is me for my hurt! ... **For the pastors are become brutish, and have not sought the Lord**" (Jeremiah 10:19-22)

IT IS THE Lord who is crying: "Woe is me for my hurt! my wound is grievous: ... **For the pastors are become brutish, and have not sought the Lord**: ..." (Jeremiah 10:19-22–emphasis added).

The pastors have betrayed us. They have sought after men, and not the Lord. Their churches have a name that they live, but in fact they are dead (Revelation 3:1). They prosper materially, but spiritually they are *poor, wretched, naked,* and *blind* and don't know it (Revelation 3:17). Consequently, the Lord's sheep are scattered and many are tangled up in new cart churches—churches that have left the old paths.

To fully appreciate what follows, we must clarify some things we touched upon earlier.

Remember, by the time that Jesus came into the world, Satan had been given power over all the kingdoms of the world (Luke 4:5-6). Jesus broke the power of Satan in the earth, cast him out, and spoiled all principalities and powers so that all power (authority) in Heaven and in earth was transferred to Him (John 12:31; Colossians 1:16;

2:15; Matthew 28:18). Satan is now the "prince and the power of the air" and operates in this world through the "children of disobedience" (Ephesians 2:1-2).

Jesus Christ has authority over the kingdom of Heaven and all the kingdoms of the earth. He has given the keys of the kingdom to His church (Matthew 16:19). In part, this means the church has the key for entrance into Christ's kingdom. That key is the gospel, which when believed allows the sinner to be translated into the kingdom of God's dear Son (Colossians 1:13). Christ manifests Himself in this world through the mortal flesh of believers, extending His authority in the earth through them (II Corinthians 4:11) as His ambassadors (II Corinthians 5:10).

The fact that Jesus has received all power in Heaven and in earth (Matthew 28:18) means that He is the ordaining power presiding over all civil authority in the earth today (Romans 13:1-6). He gives "the kingdom" (that is, the right and privilege to rule under Him) to whomever He will (Matthew 21:43; Daniel 4:17 with John 1:1, 14).

We notice that the King of Heaven and earth walks in the midst of the churches (Revelation 1:20-2:1). He is not represented as walking in the midst of the capitals, or the halls of the United Nations. As LORD of all the earth, He is keenly interested in what is going on with His churches. Why?

He gave to His churches the *keys of the kingdom.* This means the church has been given the message that grants access to the kingdom of Jesus Christ (Colossians 1:12-15; Matthew 24:14). It also means that His church is the headquarters for His ambassadors here to represent the King of kings to the nations. The churches declare the authority and Lordship of Jesus Christ the Son of God to all the nations of the earth (Matthew 28:18-20).

We send forth the command of God to all men everywhere to repent and believe on Christ Jesus (Acts 17:30). We declare that if any man will confess with his mouth the LORD Jesus, and believe in his heart that God raised Him from the dead, he will be saved (Romans 10:9). We announce to the world that all who refuse to obey the gospel command to repent and believe will be destroyed in the flaming fire of His vengeance (II Thessalonians 1:8).

Indeed, the Spirit of Christ (means the anointed One, identifies Jesus as rightful King of Heaven and earth) moves through us into the world (John 7:38-39). Christ's Spirit through us reproves the world of sin, righteousness, and judgment (John 16:7-9). All who humble themselves and repent will be blessed. Whatever blessing Christ has for the nations He extends to those nations through the gospel of the kingdom.

Since the church holds the keys of the kingdom, in order for Satan to regain his place in the earth, he must do it by infiltrating the churches. Before Satan can take hold of a nation, he must neutralize the influence of Christ's churches in that nation. (This explains the irrational hatred against Christians everywhere in the world where darkness prevails.)

Satan's favorite method to compromise God's people is Baalism, which is modern day ecumenicism. The ecumenical spirit blurs the distinction between truth and error and right and wrong, by blurring the distinctions between the children of obedience (those who obeyed the gospel from the heart) and the children of disobedience (those who reject the gospel command to repent and believe on Jesus Christ as LORD).

Pastors who succumb to the seduction of ecumenicism are modern day prophets of Baal. Jeremiah said they are brutish. This means they are animal-like, spiritually speaking. They are of this "earth, earthy" (I Corinthians 15:47). Their wisdom does not descend from above, but it is earthly, sensual, and devilish (James 3:15). With cunning craftiness, they deceive the simple among God's people (Ephesians 4:14). They are the "evil men and seducers" the Spirit warned us would "wax worse and worse, deceiving, and being deceived" (II Timothy 3:13). Satan transforms himself into an angel of light (II Corinthians 11:14), and his ministers are "transformed as the ministers of righteousness" (II Corinthians 11:15). They compromise the Word of God to gain favor with the world of men.

God proclaimed that because the pastors have become brutish, the sheep of His pasture are scattered from Him. The consequence of this is that judgment comes upon their nation from a strange nation. Their cities become desolate and overrun with devils. In other words, when Christ's appointed evangelists and pastor–teachers start concerning themselves with tickling the ears of the people instead of feeding Christ's sheep, the sheep stray from the old paths of God's ways into paths that lead to divine judgment upon them.

Before I conclude this part and move on to describe what a new cart church looks like and offer insight on how to make your way back into the old paths, we must consider one more matter. True, God blames His pastors for this, but His children are not entirely free of responsibility. God searches their hearts and says, "The prophets prophesy falsely, and the priests bear rule by their means; and my people love to have it so…" (Jeremiah 5:31). *My people love to have it so!* God blames the pastors for submitting to the pressure backslidden believers place on them to compromise. But He laments with a broken heart: "And my people are bent to backsliding from me…" (Hosea 11:7).

In the next several chapters I will make clear the differences between an old path church and a new cart church, and show you how you can find your way back into the old paths.

Chapter Five

The Right Foundation

JESUS SAID, "I WILL build *my* church" (Matthew 16:18– emphasis added). Jesus is the Word (John 1:1-14). He would do nothing contrary to His Father's will (Hebrews 10:9). God's will is revealed to us through His Word. A church that is built by Jesus Christ will be built according to His Word. Let's consider some things the Bible says that can help us identify the church that Jesus promised to build.

Jesus said He would build His church upon the *rock:* Matthew 16:18, "Upon this rock I will build my church."

Some think "this rock" is Peter. In Matthew 16:18, the Greek word translated *Peter* is transliterated *petros*, but the word translated *rock* is *petras*. *Petros* is masculine and *petras* is feminine. The word *petros* is used to speak of a piece of rock. The feminine form (*petras*) is used to speak of that mass of rock from which a piece of rock would come.

This agrees perfectly with Ephesians 2:20, where we learn that the foundation upon which the church is built is composed of Jesus

Christ, the Chief Cornerstone, combined with the apostles and prophets (Ephesians 2:20). All 12 Apostles of the Lamb are included as part of the foundation of the church (Revelation 21:14). If the foundation of the church is Jesus Christ as the Chief Cornerstone together with the apostles and the prophets, then Peter is not the rock upon which the church is built; he is only one part of the foundation that is built upon the rock. A foundation must rest upon something. Jesus would build His house on rock, and not on sand (Matthew 7:24-26). What is the rock upon which the foundation is laid?

Many believe the rock upon which Jesus said He would build His church is Peter's testimony concerning Jesus: "Thou art the Christ, the Son of the living God" (Matthew 16:16). Others believe Jesus was referring to Peter as a rock that Jesus would place upon The Rock, which is Christ (I Corinthians 10:4). Both of these arguments lead to the same conclusion. Jesus is the Rock on which the church is built. According to Paul the Apostle ultimately Jesus Christ is the only foundation upon which a church can be built (I Corinthians 3:9-11). The foundation of any structure includes the ground upon which the foundation is built. Jesus is the Rock upon which the foundation of the church is built (I Corinthians 10:4; Ephesians 2:20).

The question is how can we know whether a church rests upon the right foundation?

Jesus Christ is the Rock upon which the foundation of the church is laid and the Chief Cornerstone in that foundation. He is the Word incarnate. That means He is the Word made flesh (John 1:1,14; I Timothy 3:16). The church is built upon God's Word.

The written Word of God is called the Scripture (John 10:35). All Scripture is given by the inspiration of God (II Timothy 3:16). The word translated *inspiration* means *God breathed out.* Peter explained inspiration of the Holy Scripture happened when the Holy Ghost moved holy men of God to speak exactly what God wanted them to say (II Peter 1:20-21).

Peter referred to the writings of the Apostle Paul as Scripture (II Peter 3:16). Indeed, all the New Testament was given to us by the

Spirit of Christ through Christ's apostles or by men of God writing under their authority.

The church is built upon the apostles and prophets. The Spirit of Christ gave us the Old Testament Scriptures through the prophets (I Peter 1:11). The apostles' instruction is communicated to us in the New Testament. Christ's Spirit is the Spirit Who inspired them to write, and Christ is the Chief Cornerstone of this foundation. Therefore, the foundation of a church is proved by its submission to the authority of the words of the Word. If a church rejects the authority of the Scriptures, it is not resting on the right foundation. It is not a church that Jesus built.

Some will argue that the church is built upon the Name of the Lord Jesus Christ and not upon His Holy Spirit inspired Scriptures. Indeed, there is no other name given among men whereby we must be saved (Acts 4:12). And every knee shall bow, and every tongue shall confess that Name before the Holy Father at His coming (Romans 14:11; Philippians 2:10). However, the Spirit declares that God has magnified His Word "above all his name" (Psalm 138:2). Anyone can claim His Name (Matthew 7:22), but Jesus will acknowledge only those who submit to the authority of His Word (Matthew 15:8; Mark 8:38; John 8:31-37; 12:48; 14:23; 15:7). The test of fellowship is not His Name, but the words of His Word—the Scripture.

If a church is not set upon the right foundation, you can be certain that Jesus Christ is not building it. Paul said, "Other foundation can no man lay than that is laid, which is Jesus Christ" (I Corinthians 3:11). Jesus Christ is the Word incarnated. The Word of God (the Bible) is the Word of God breathed out by His Spirit through Holy men of God into the Holy Scriptures. By some this is called the Word *inscripturated*. To reject the authority of the word inscripturated is to reject the authority of the Word incarnated. Any church that denies the Word of God, or rejects the authority of the apostles and prophets is not a church that is built by Jesus Christ.

Let's consider one simple but effective test you can use to determine whether your church is built upon the right foundation

Most believers who consider themselves conservative, Bible-believing Christians would agree with the following statement: a true church must be built upon the teachings of God's Holy Word given by the inspiration of God and found in the Bible. But did you know that most churches today use Bible versions that ascribe to Satan a title that belongs exclusively to Jesus Christ?

Open your Bible to Isaiah 14:12. The passage is obviously about Satan. If your version identifies Satan as *day–star, Daystar, Day Star, morning star,* or *star of the morning,* you have a Bible that ascribes to Satan a title that belongs exclusively to Jesus Christ:

> "We have also a more sure word of prophecy; whereunto ye do well that ye take heed, as unto a light that shineth in a dark place, until the day dawn, and the day star arise in your hearts" (II Peter 1:19). (In the context of II Peter 1:19, the expression *day star* is a reference to Jesus Christ.)

> "I Jesus have sent mine angel to testify unto you these things in the churches. I am the root and the offspring of David, and the bright and morning star" (Revelation 22:16). (Jesus identifies Himself as the *morning star.*)

Any version that uses the title *Day Star, morning star,* or the equivalent in Isaiah 14:12 is giving to Satan a title that belongs to Jesus Christ.

Is there any justification for this translation? No!

In the King James Bible, Isaiah 14:12 says, "How art thou fallen from Heaven, O Lucifer, son of the morning! how art thou cut down to the ground, which didst weaken the nations!"

The Hebrew word that is translated *Lucifer* is found only once in Scripture and cannot be found in any literature outside of the Hebrew Scriptures. It is a proper noun made from a Hebrew verb that means *to howl* (Strong No. 3213). It is pronounced *heylel* (Strong No. 1966), which sounds similar to another Hebrew word, *halel* (Strong No. 1984). Halel means *praise.* Heylel means *one who howls* or *yells.* Because of the similarity in the sound of these words, some think heylel is a modification of halel, and suggest it signifies that Satan who was once God's praise was demoted and became the howling one.

Although the idea that heylel is a modification of halel is mere conjecture, we know that Satan was at one time the *praise of God* (Ezekiel 28:12-15). However, because of his pride he was cast down and became the howling or yelling one. In the passage of Isaiah where he is given this unique name he is seen howling against God in the anguish of his anger and shame. It is a fitting name for Satan.

Were the translators of the Authorized Version correct to use *Lucifer* to translate Heylel in Isaiah 14:12? They recognized that the word *Heylel* was coined from the Hebrew verb *to howl* creating a unique proper name for Satan. The English proper name for Satan then in common use was *Lucifer.* It suits that howling Devil who transforms himself into an angel of light (II Corinthians 11:14). I believe all of the meaning that God breathed (inspired) through the word *Heylel* is expressed in the word *Lucifer.*

In Strong's Concordance, the meaning you will find ascribed to the Hebrew word translated *Lucifer* comes entirely from an assumption about that Latin word, which, some say, signifies shining. This is the basis for including the word *star* in many of the newer translations. The problem with this theory is that there is nothing to support it. In fact, there is nothing at all in the Hebrew of Isaiah 14 that refers to a star (Strong No. 3556, *kowkab*). The reference to Satan as *son of the morning* acknowledges only that he was among the "sons of God" that shouted at the dawn of creation (Job 38:7). There is no justification for using "morning star" for anything in Isaiah 14.

Nothing can justify ascribing to Satan, God's enemy, a title the Bible gives exclusively to Jesus Christ, God's Son.

How did such a thing occur, and why do so many seemingly good Christian people accept these versions? The simple answer is this, "My people are destroyed for lack of knowledge" (Hosea 4:6).

The Bible warns that some would depart from the faith, giving heed to "seducing spirits, teaching doctrines of devils" (I Timothy 4:1). We are commanded not to believe every spirit, but to try the spirits to see if they are of God (I John 4:1-2). What spirit do you suppose would contrive to give to Satan a title that belongs exclusively to Jesus Christ?

The Word of God is foundational to the church. Jesus, the Word of God incarnate, builds His church upon the Scriptures, the words of the Word inscripturated. It is very obvious that Jesus has nothing to do with the building of churches that use a Bible that calls Satan by a title that belongs to Him alone.

Many churches proclaim the Name of Jesus Christ, but they have adopted Bible versions that are clearly of another spirit. They might desire to be an authentic Christian church. They might desire to do the right thing. But they have they have adopted Bible versions that have been corrupted. What you will notice is that virtually every church that uses one of these corrupt Bible versions will manifest most if not all of the characteristics of the new cart church, which I will continue to define in upcoming chapters.

One way to identify a new cart church is by the Bible version(s) that they use. But that is not the only concern. It is possible for a church to be built upon the right foundation, and yet to come under the control and influence of the spirit of the world (I Corinthians 2:12).

Chapter Six

Discerning the Spirit of a Ministry

T HE BIBLE WARNS US, "Beloved, believe not every spirit, but try the spirits whether they are of God" (I John 4:1). It is possible for a church to come under the power and influence of another spirit and not know it. For example, Jesus once rebuked the disciples: "Ye know not what manner of spirit ye are of" (Luke 9:55). Indeed, I John 4:1 is a warning of the possibility that other spirits can gain an influence in our lives. Paul warned that "seducing spirits" and "doctrines of devils" would lead many into error (I Timothy 4:1-2). For this reason, we are warned not to believe every spirit, but to try them to see if they are of God. If Christ's own disciples confessed Jesus Christ is come in the flesh and were very active in evangelistic ministry and yet occasionally came under the power of another spirit, it is possible for churches that confess Jesus Christ and preach the gospel to come under the influence of other spirits and to not even be aware of it.

There are three general tests you can use to discern if your church has come under the power and influence of a false spirit.

The first test: What is the confession of the church concerning Jesus Christ? If any church does not confess that Jesus Christ is come in the flesh, then that church is not of God (I John 4:3).

The second test: Does the church preach the true gospel and does it have a passion for seeking the salvation of the lost? Paul, by the Spirit, warned of those who might come preaching *another Jesus,* motivated by *another spirit,* declaring *another gospel* (II Corinthians 11:4). He lamented that the believers in Galatia had turned from the "grace of Christ unto another gospel" (Galatians 1:6). Jesus was guided by the Holy Spirit in all that He did, and He came to "seek and to save that which was lost" (Luke 19:10). He gave us His Spirit with the charge to preach His gospel to everyone everywhere in the world (Mark 16:15; Luke 24:46-49; Acts 1:5-8). Later, I'll be giving very particular attention to the issue of the true gospel, and the difference between genuine old path evangelism and the new cart variety. Suffice it here to point out that no church can claim to be led of the Spirit of Christ that does not preach the true gospel, and that does not have a passion for reaching all mankind with the gospel.

The third test: Is the church following the leadership of the Holy Spirit? The Holy Spirit was sent into the world to do specific things. If these things do not characterize your church's ministry then your church is not following the Holy Spirit.

Jesus said the Holy Spirit was sent into the world to reprove it of sin, righteousness, and judgment (John 16:8). A few verses later, He added that the Spirit was sent to "guide [us] into all truth" (John 16:13). In John 17:17 Jesus said, "Thy word is truth." Therefore we expect the Spirit to guide us to truth in God's Word, the Bible. Additionally, the Spirit was sent to hold believers together in unity and to produce in them the fruit of love, joy, peace, longsuffering, gentleness, goodness, faith, meekness, and temperance (Ephesians 4:3; Galatians 5:22-23).

If a church is not reproving the world of sin, righteousness, and judgment it is not following the Holy Spirit; it is following another spirit. If a church is not keenly interested in the truth and searching the Scriptures for the truth, or if it is rejecting any plain teaching of Scripture, then that church is not following the Spirit of Christ. They are of another spirit. If a church is characteristically divisive, unloving, impatient with weak brethren or sinners, harsh, full of bad behavior, without faith, and intemperate, that church is not one that is guided by the Holy Spirit. Such churches have come under the control of another spirit.

In the following chapters, I'll present fourteen questions you can use to discern whether the church you are evaluating is under the influence of the Holy Spirit, or of some other spirit.

Chapter Seven

A Praying Church

Question One: *Does the church make prayer a top priority!*

JESUS SAID, "IS IT not written, My house shall be called of all nations the house of prayer?" (Mark 11:17; Isaiah 56:7) The Temple was the house of God and God wanted His house to be known as the house of prayer.

Today, the church is the house of God: "But if I tarry long, that thou mayest know how thou oughtest to behave thyself in the house of God, which is the church of the living God, the pillar and ground of the truth" (I Timothy 3:15). What He said concerning His house in the Old Testament now applies to His church. The Father wants His church to be known among all men as "the house of prayer." Any church that is following the Spirit of truth will take prayer seriously. In fact, they will make prayer a priority.

Indeed, the Apostle Paul said *prayer was first of all*: "I exhort therefore, that, first of all, supplications, prayers, intercessions, and giving of thanks, be made for all men" (I Timothy 2:1). Yet today, most Christians make prayer last of all.

Churches are known for many different things. Some are known for their good works in a community. Others are known for their stand on doctrine, or the preaching and teaching of their leaders, or on their focus on soulwinning, or their passion for missions. Some are well known for their dynamic worship services, and still others are known for their friendliness. Every church should desire to be known as possessing all of these characteristics, yet the most important thing to be known for is prayer.[21] Unfortunately, that is usually the last thing people think about when they evaluate a church.

We are specifically concerned with helping Christ's sheep discern between an old path and a new cart church. The sad truth is that there is very little difference between an old path church and a new cart church when it comes the importance each places on prayer. So why do I present this as the first question you should ask when attempting to discern whether a ministry is guided by the Holy Ghost?

The first reason is because although a church may be a very sound, old path church, it will degenerate away from the LORD if the pastors and the people do not pray.

The second reason is that prayer is the first step God commands us to take. Remember that the prophet Jeremiah counseled the people in his day to, "Stand in the ways, and ask for the old paths" (Jeremiah 6:16b). He is saying, in effect, *stop what you are doing, look at the ways before you, and ask Me to guide you to the old paths where is the good way* (Jeremiah 6:16). When we ask God to show us the old paths, we are praying. We must begin with prayer because that is the first step commanded by God.

---

21 Oh, how I long to expand on this vital point. As the executive editor for *The Intercessor* magazine, as well as an advisory board member for Intercessor Ministries, I have firsthand experience, and inside-the-ministry insights, into the spiritual warfare that rages all about us and the vital role that prayer plays in that war (Ephesians 6:10-19). However, because that goes beyond the purpose of this book, I recommend that you read the most important contemporary book written on the subject of prayer: <u>Prayer for Revival</u>, by Dr. Benny Beckum, famous prayer evangelist, founder and president of Intercessor Ministries, and publisher of *The Intercessor*. Everyone interested in prayer should subscribe to *The Intercessor*. Another helpful resource available through Intercessor Ministries is the book <u>Kingdom Power by Prayer and Fasting</u>.

Practically speaking, when we pray for direction, we submit our spirit to the Spirit of truth, Who was given to us to guide us to all truth (John 16:13). Since, as Jesus said, "Thy word is truth," (John 17:17), we prayerfully study the Scriptures for the direction we need to find the old paths for which we have prayed.

The third reason I begin with prayer is that the pastors' failure to pray was the first step leading them and their flocks out of the old paths: "For the pastors are become brutish, and have not sought the LORD" (Jeremiah 10:21a). A man's heart leaves the way of the LORD long before his feet do. The departure began with a failure to pray and so the return begins with restoring a prayer life.

The fourth reason is because a church that does not understand the importance of prayer will leave believers to wander in the spiritual wilderness, scattered from the LORD: "therefore they shall not prosper, and all their flocks shall be scattered" (Jeremiah 10:21b).

The fifth reason is the most important reason of all. We must begin with prayer because the revival that is needed today is a prayer revival. And today, a prayer revival of a very peculiar kind is what is particularly needed. We need the prayer revival modeled by Elijah the prophet (I Kings 17-19). And unless a church is a praying church, it will not stand as God's Elijah to challenge the modern prophets of Baal to the coming prayer duel.

Elijah was the leading prophet of God in the days that the priestess of Zidon, Jezebel, had prevailed to establish the religion of Baalism throughout Israel. Many of Elijah's fellow prophets had abandoned the old paths of their fathers and joined in preaching the ecumenism of Jezebel. These were called the prophets of the groves (I Kings 18:19). Those who would not compromise and join Jezebel in her effort to unite all the religions of the regions together under Baal were killed, or they hid from Jezebel in Obadiah's cave (I Kings 18:4, 13). Elijah was a lonely prophet (I Kings 18:22)!

As I've explained earlier, Baalism taught that everyone worshiped the same God only by different names and in different forms. The only religious idea that was considered objectionable was the notion that there is only one God to the exclusion of all others. In this religious milieu, it became impossible to distinguish between the true worshipers of Jehovah and those who served Baal.

But even in Jezebel's Israel, God had a small remnant dispersed throughout the land, 7,000, to be exact, who had not bowed the knee to Baal, or kissed him (Romans 11:4; I Kings 19:18). It seems likely that this remnant cried out to God for a revival that would restore their nation to His blessing and favor.

However, God could not extend His blessing upon the nation while so many had turned their hearts away from Him and followed after Baal. For one reason, if He did send a revival to His people, the prophets of Baal and the prophets of the groves, and Jezebel herself, would no doubt take the credit for the blessings and point to them as confirmation of their religion. No doubt the prophets of Jezebel from Zidon would boast that the blessings were coming on account of their prayers to Ashtoreth, the Baal of the Zidonians, while the prophets of the groves would boast the blessings were coming from their prayers to their Baal, Jehovah of Hosts. But God is a jealous God (Exodus 20:5; 34:14; Deuteronomy 4:24; 5:9; 6:15; Joshua 24:19). He will not share His glory with another (Isaiah 42:8; 48:11).

God determined that He would show Israel Who is the true and only God, and which among the prophets was His. He did this by instructing Elijah to challenge the Baalites to a prayer duel (I Kings 18:17-38). Elijah called them all to Mount Carmel where he would present the challenge.

Elijah cried: "How long halt ye between two opinions? if the LORD be God, follow him: but if Baal, then follow him" (I Kings 18:21). Then he set before them the challenge. Each side would present an offering before their respective deity and the deity that answered by fire would be acknowledged as the true God. The people accepted the challenge.

The prophets of the multi-faced Baal were instructed to lay their wood upon their altar (I Kings 18:26), to set their bullock upon the wood, and to put no fire under it. Then they were to pray to their

Baal, that is, call upon their gods (I Kings 18:24). Those of Zidon would pray to Baal by the name of Ashtoreth. Those of Moab would pray to Chemosh. Those of Ammon would call on Milcom. Interestingly, the prophets of the groves, who called their Baal by the name Jehovah, were not invited to participate. Only the 450 prophets of Baal were invited to pray, while the 400 prophets of the groves were left standing there to watch (I Kings 18:19, 22).

The Baalites prayed with zeal and in earnest (I Kings 18:26), "Oh Baal, hear us," leaping upon the altar they had made. Elijah mocked them: "Cry aloud: for he is a god; either he is talking, or he is pursuing, or he is in a journey, or peradventure he sleepeth, and must be awaked" (I Kings 18:27). They responded with even greater fervor, going so far as to cut themselves with knives and lancets so that their blood gushed from them onto their altar (I Kings 18:28).

None answered! Then it was Elijah's turn.

He repaired the forgotten, and broken down, old path altar of the LORD (I Kings 18:30). Then he rededicated it distinctly as the altar of Israel, differentiating it from the altars of Baal (I Kings 18:31-32). He dug a trench around the altar and then set the sacrifice upon the wood. He instructed that they pour water over the sacrifice, soaking it and the wood and filling the trench. No one would be able to say Elijah had stealthily put some fire under the wood of the sacrifice. Then Elijah prayed a simple, humble, and short prayer: "LORD God of Abraham, Isaac, and of Israel, let it be known this day that thou art God in Israel, and that I am thy servant, and that I have done all these things at thy word. Hear me, O LORD, hear me, that this people may know that thou art the LORD God, and that thou hast turned their heart back again" (I Kings 18:36-7).

God answered! The fire fell! And the people shouted: "The LORD He is the God; the LORD, He is the God" (I Kings 18:39).

In that prayer duel, God showed Who He is, differentiating Himself from all the rest. He openly identified which congregation was His, and which prophet He honored. God used a prayer revival to turn the people back into the old paths.

The Bible indicates that God was about to judge that nation, but on behalf of a faithful remnant, God raised up an Elijah who led a prayer revival that extended the kingdom for nearly 200 years. This is the revival that we need today.

I mentioned earlier that there was a day when almost any church could put out a sign calling on their neighbors to stop in and join them in prayer, and God would honor this with great revivals. The great revival of 1801 began in New York with an advertisement in the local newspaper inviting the general public to a prayer meeting. Jeremy Lanphier placed the advertisement inviting anyone interested to join him at a rented hall on Fulton Street, in New York. Only six responded to that invitation. But before long, a general outpouring of God's Spirit came down on the believers in New York and a great revival broke out.[22] Those days are long past.

Ecumenical prayer meetings are so common today that the general public ignores them as virtually meaningless. Ecumenical national days of prayer are called, almost routinely, and nothing comes of it. God will not bless the prayers of the Baalites, even if the prophets of the groves, the compromising evangelical pastors, join them. The prayers of Mormons holding hands with Catholics and their compromised evangelical prophets of the groves will never be answered by the God and Father of our Lord Jesus Christ with revival fire.

For conclusion, I want to add a note regarding the current state of things, how I'm praying about it, and what is needed today.

I believe we are under the curse of Isaiah 50:11. In that verse, God said, "Behold, all ye that kindle a fire, that compass yourselves about with sparks: walk in the light of your fire, and in the sparks that ye have kindled. This shall ye have of mine hand; ye shall lie down in sorrow." That's where we are today. These new cart pastors kindle a great many false fires, and generate a lot of sparks, but our nation is forsaken of God's blessing and we lie down in sorrow. When you read the next verse (Isaiah 50:12) you will see that the answer is always the same; return to the old paths, "Hearken to me, ye that

---

22 http://www.christianity.com/church/church-history/timeline/1801-1900/jeremy-lanphier-led-prayer-revival-11630507.html (2/5/14)

follow after righteousness, ye that seek the LORD: look unto the rock whence ye are hewn, and to the hole of the pit whence ye are digged," that is, return to your roots.

Evil spirits operate in this world and they are dedicated to seducing God's people away from the old paths (I Timothy 4:1; I John 4:1). However, the Bible tells us that greater is He that is in us than he that is in the world (I John 4:4). In other words, the Holy Spirit in us is greater than the spirit of antichrist that operates in the world (Ephesians 2:2). In fact, the Bible teaches that the Holy Spirit in us withholds the spirit of antichrist from achieving its purpose in the world today (II Thessalonians 2:7). Yet, when we grieve or quench the Spirit of God (Ephesians 4:30-31; I Thessalonians 5:19), we empower the evil spirits to seduce God's people away from Him and to strengthen their evil influence in the world. When this happens, it allows the evil spirits to work wonders in the earth that are very deceptive (Matthew 24:24; Revelation 13:14; 19:20).

False worshipers sacrifice to devils, and by this, perhaps unwittingly, they worship them (I Corinthians 10:20; Revelation 9:20). And such devils can affect a kind of fire and generate a kind of spark that look like holy fire. Satan is an imitator, after all (II Corinthians 11:14).

What we need today is someone with the ear of God, and a walk with God like Elijah had, whose prayers will be heard so that God will reverse the curse of Isaiah 50:11 that I perceive is upon us. Only then will the devils be restrained from allowing these false preachers to deceive the Lord's sheep with their false fire and sparks.

God's true prophets must come out from hiding in the caves, and join the few Elijahs who stand alone against the ecumenical spirit. They must repair the prayer altars, and set the wood, the Cross, in order. They must lay upon this altar their body a living sacrifice, holy and acceptable unto God (Romans 12:1-2). Then the water of God's Word must be repeatedly poured over the sacrifice till every ember bearing in it any of Baal's false fire, and every false spark of fleshly pretensions to holiness, is extinguished.

I pray that God will indeed frustrate the Baalites, that no devils will be able to mock answered prayers. I pray that every effort at an ecumenical prayer meeting will be exposed manifestly as an exercise in vanity. That whatever remnant there might be remaining in this country will be called out of the new cart churches, and into the old path churches, where God will hear us indeed, and grant a reviving in our land.

It is important that you find a church that emphasizes prayer. However, remember that the Baalites believed in prayer and prayed with great zeal. Furthermore, remember that many old path churches have allowed the prayer altar to be broken down and neglected. Checking the church's commitment to prayer is an essential concern, but it is not the only concern.

Chapter Eight

A Proper Regard for Doctrine

Question Two: *Does the church have a proper regard for doctrine?*

THE EMPHASIS PLACED BY the apostles on the importance of doctrine is ignored by most who call themselves Christians today. Yet, even a cursory survey of verses that speak to the importance of doctrine will immediately show that these Christians are of a different spirit than the One Who inspired these Scriptures:

Acts 2:42 And they continued stedfastly in the apostles' **doctrine** and fellowship, and in breaking of bread, and in prayers.

Romans 6:17 But God be thanked, that ye were the servants of sin, but ye have obeyed from the heart that form of **doctrine** which was delivered you.

Romans 16:17 Now I beseech you, brethren, mark them which cause divisions and offences contrary to the **doctrine** which ye have learned; and avoid them.

Ephesians 4:14 That we *henceforth* be no more children, tossed to and fro, and carried about with every wind of **doctrine**, by the sleight of men, *and* cunning craftiness, whereby they lie in wait to deceive.

I Timothy 1:3 As I besought thee to abide still at Ephesus, when I went into Macedonia, that thou mightest charge some that they teach no other **doctrine**.

I Timothy 1:10 For whoremongers, for them that defile themselves with mankind, for menstealers, for liars, for perjured persons, and if there be any other thing that is contrary to sound **doctrine**.

I Timothy 4:6 If thou put the brethren in remembrance of these things, thou shalt be a good minister of Jesus Christ, nourished up in the words of faith and of good **doctrine**, whereunto thou hast attained.

I Timothy 4:13 Till I come, give attendance to reading, to exhortation, to **doctrine**.

I Timothy 4:16 Take heed unto thyself, and unto the **doctrine**; continue in them: for in doing this thou shalt both save thyself, and them that hear thee.

I Timothy 5:17 Let the elders that rule well be counted worthy of double honour, especially they who labour in the word and **doctrine**.

I Timothy 6:1 Let as many servants as are under the yoke count their own masters worthy of all honour, that the name of God and *his* **doctrine** be not blasphemed.

I Timothy 6:3 If any man teach otherwise, and consent not to wholesome words, *even* the words of our Lord Jesus Christ, and to the **doctrine** which is according to godliness.

II Timothy 3:10 But thou hast fully known my **doctrine**, manner of life, purpose, faith, longsuffering, charity, patience...

II Timothy 3:16 All scripture *is* given by inspiration of God, and *is* profitable for **doctrine**, for reproof, for correction, for instruction in righteousness.

II Timothy 4:2 Preach the word; be instant in season, out of season; reprove, rebuke, exhort with all longsuffering and **doctrine**.

Titus 1:9 Holding fast the faithful word as he hath been taught, that he may be able by sound **doctrine** both to exhort and to convince the gainsayers.

Titus 2:1 But speak thou the things which become sound **doctrine**.

Titus 2:7 In all things shewing thyself a pattern of good works: in **doctrine** *shewing* uncorruptness, gravity, sincerity.

Titus 2:10 Not purloining, but shewing all good fidelity; that they may adorn the **doctrine** of God our Saviour in all things.

II John 9 Whosoever transgresseth, and abideth not in the **doctrine** of Christ, hath not God. He that abideth in the doctrine of Christ, he hath both the Father and the Son.

II John 10 If there come any unto you, and bring not this **doctrine**, receive him not into *your* house, neither bid him God speed.

Revelation 2:14 But I have a few things against thee, because thou hast there them that hold the **doctrine** of Balaam, who taught Balac to cast a stumblingblock before the children of Israel, to eat things sacrificed unto idols, and to commit fornication.

Revelation 2:15 So hast thou also them that hold the **doctrine** of the Nicolaitans, which thing I hate.

Revelation 2:24 But unto you I say, and unto the rest in Thyatira, as many as have not this **doctrine**, and which have not known the depths of Satan, as they speak; I will put upon you none other burden.

Even the verses that warn against false doctrine show the importance of getting our doctrine right. No believer indwelt by the Holy Ghost can read the above verses without being impressed with the fact that doctrine is important to God. Clearly, the Holy Spirit Who inspired the above Scripture passages would never influence any Christian to dismiss doctrine as unimportant or irrelevant or otherwise diminish the importance of doctrine. Churches that dismiss doctrine as unimportant are not of the Spirit of Christ; they are of another spirit.

Chapter Nine

A Ministry of Reproof

Question Three: *Does the church have a ministry that delivers the Holy Spirit's reproof to the world?*

CHURCHES TODAY GO OUT of their way to present themselves as friends with the world (James 4:4). Usually they justify following this seducing spirit by pointing out that Jesus was a friend of sinners (Matthew 11:19; Luke 7:34). It is like Satan to use Scriptures taken out of context to confuse believers (Matthew 4:6-7). If you read the verses where Jesus is called a friend of sinners you will notice this was a slanderous accusation hurled at Him by His enemies. True, He loved sinners so much He died for us all on the Cross. However, Jesus was not a friend of sinners in the sense that He sought their company, or consorted with them, or walked in their way, or engaged in their sinful activities with them. On the contrary, the Spirit of Christ through His apostles repeatedly calls Christ's disciples to separate from sinners (II Corinthians 6:17; I Corinthians 5:9-13).

I do not mean you cannot talk to sinners, or dine with them, or invite them to a meal in hopes to witness to them. Read Matthew 9:11; Mark 2:16; and Luke 15:2. In each of these cases Jesus dined with sinners. But this did not mean He was consorting with known drunkards, fornicators, or thieves (I Corinthians 5:10). (Consider the example of Zacchaeus (Luke 19:5-9).) My meaning is clear. We are not to join with them in their sinful activities, or follow after their sinful lifestyle, or connect ourselves with them in any way that would give the appearance that we approve of their behavior or that we are ambivalent regarding it. Neither do we avoid reproving them for fear of offending them. If the activities of a church do not result in the Spirit reproving the conscience of your community of sin, righteousness, and judgment, the Spirit of Christ is not leading that church. It is under the influence of another spirit.

Consider some examples from the Lord Jesus Christ.

A Samaritan woman came to Jacob's well to draw water. Jesus asked her to draw some water for Him, and in the course of the banter that followed, He offered to give her water that if she would drink she would never thirst again (John 4:4-26). When she asked Him, "Sir, give me this water, that I thirst not, neither come hither to draw" (John 4:15), Jesus abruptly changed the subject. He instructed her to go get her husband. When she said she had no husband, Jesus said, "Thou hast well said, I have no husband: for thou hast had five husbands; and he whom thou now hast is not thy husband: in that saidst thou truly" (John 4:16-18). By this she recognized He was a prophet, and soon she came to see that He was her Messiah (John 4:24-26). However, before she could receive the water of life, she had to be confronted with the truth about her sinful life.

If a new cart Christian brings up the issue of sin, it is brought up in so generic and abstract a manner as to be meaningless. They might say, "Well, of course, as you know, we are all sinners." Or, "I'm a sinner, just like you." And quote "For all have sinned and come short of the glory of God" (Romans 3:23). It's easy to confess you are a generic sinner, but it's something else to be confronted with specific sins that provoke the heart to experience shame or guilt. Rather than provoke the conscience of sinners to experience godly sorrow leading to repentance, new cart Christians actually reinforce the hardness of their heart over their sin and dismiss the issue as relatively unimportant.

When a certain Gentile woman approached Jesus to heal her daughter, He spoke to her in a manner that would be shocking to virtually every new cart Christian (Matthew 15:22-28). She was a woman of Canaan who came to Him for help for her daughter who was sick. Jesus at first seemed to ignore her. But she continued pleading. His disciples begged Him to send her away, but instead Jesus said to them, "I am not sent but unto the lost sheep of the house of Israel" (Matthew 15:24). Falling down and worshiping Him she pleaded with Him to heal her sick daughter. Jesus spoke directly to her said, "It is not meet to take the children's bread and to cast it to dogs" (Matthew 15:26). Finally she cried, "Truth, Lord: yet the dogs eat of the crumbs that fall from their master's table" (Matthew 15:27). Jesus marveled at her extraordinary faith and rewarded her with the petition she desired of Him.

I think any Christian who knows Christ Jesus understands that He was purposely drawing this faith out of the heart of this pagan woman. But the point here is that Jesus did indeed challenge her faith; He used the Law of God to reprove her and humble her heart, and then she was saved. Some might object that Jesus is an exception, and we cannot expect to pattern our witnessing after His example. But that is a mistake. First, we are specifically told to walk in His steps (I Peter 2:21). Second, if the Spirit that guided Him guides us, should not we expect to be guided in the same way?

Sometimes the sinner is already repentant, and it is therefore not necessary to confront them with their personal sins. One of my favorite stories in the Gospel of John is of the woman who was taken in adultery by the Scribes and Pharisees and cast down at Jesus' feet demanding that He stone her to death according to the Law of Moses (John 8:1-11). Jesus did not mention her sin to her. He did not reprove her. He did not show disgust for her sinfulness, or wretchedness. He knelt and wrote something on the ground with His finger while they continued demanding that He tell them whether or not He would apply the Law to her and stone her to death. He stood and said, "He that is without sin among you, let him first cast a stone at her" (John 8:7).

He did not say she did not deserve the condemnation of the Law of Moses. What He did was to apply the Law of Moses upon all of them. When their conscience humbled them, and they left, Jesus asked her if there were any remaining to accuse her. She said "No man, Lord" (John 8:11). She confessed with her mouth that Jesus is Lord (Romans 10:9). Jesus told her that neither would He stone her, and He commanded her to go "and sin no more" (John 8:10-11). Obviously, when a sinner is humbled by conviction for their sin and repentance is obvious then they have already acknowledged their sin and have humbled themselves to the righteousness of God.

How about the apostles of our Lord Jesus Christ? The rulers of the Jews resented the apostles preaching to the people in the name of Jesus. Some of these rulers of the Jews no doubt had personally participated in the crucifixion of Jesus Christ. Listen to what Peter and the other apostles said to these men:

> Then Peter and the other apostles answered and said, We ought to obey God rather than men. The God of our fathers raised up Jesus, whom ye slew and hanged on a tree. Him hath God exalted with his right hand to be a Prince and a Saviour, for to give repentance to Israel, and forgiveness of sins. (Acts 5:29-31)

Would Joel Osteen, or Rick Warren, or Bill Hybels, or even Billy Graham have said such a thing in this context? Would any of these men accuse sinners of their public sin to their face and in public? Most new cart preachers would avoid this kind of direct confrontation with sinners.

Can you imagine any new cart Christian today openly, and publicly, rebuking a sinner who was attempting to persuade someone not to listen to preaching? Well, maybe they would say something soft, like, "I really wish you would not do that" or "Don't you think they should be able to make up their own mind about whether they want to listen to us," or something along those lines. But can you imagine any new cart Christian saying, "O full of all subtilty, and all mischief, thou child of the devil, thou enemy of all righteousness, wilt thou not cease to pervert the right ways of the Lord" (Acts 13:10)?

The point of this is to get you to start thinking about something. The Spirit that moved in Jesus and the apostles is obviously very different from the spirit that influences the new cart Christian today.

Does the ministry of your church deliver a reproof upon the conscience of the sinners in your community or does your church avoid issues of sin that have been politicized by the world? If a church is not engaged in openly and publicly reproving, rebuking, and exhorting saints and sinners by the preaching of the Word of God (II Timothy 4:2) then that ministry is not guided, controlled, and influenced by the Holy Spirit. It has come under the influence and control of another spirit.

What about the sins that the world has politicized, like homosexuality and abortion? Because our government has officially rejected what the Bible says about these things, should Christians avoid confronting sinners on these matters? What about lying politicians, what about rulers who do evil, or other actions of the government that are clear violations of the laws of Christ, the King?[23] Before you can understand our responsibility to and our relationship with the kingdoms of this world, we need to understand spiritual warfare (Ephesians 6:10-19), and that is the subject of the next chapter.

------

23 I have written extensively on this subject in another work, titled *God's War!*

Chapter Ten

Engaged in Spiritual Warfare

Question Four: *Does the church engage in spiritual warfare against the spirit of antichrist manifesting in the world?*

DEVILS ARE ACTIVE IN the world today! Most believers do not understand spiritual warfare and some scorn the idea that devils are active in the world, and in the lives of Christians.[24] But they are, and the Bible is clear on this subject.

Satan exerts significant influence upon the lives of many Christians, but they are completely unaware of it. This can happen to very dedicated and sincere Christians. Remember that Peter came under the power of Satan very soon after he experienced a high point in his spiritual life (Matthew 16:17-23). If it can happen to such dedicated believers then you can be certain that it is a huge problem for weak, carnal, self-serving Christians. Take Ananias and Sapphira whose hearts Satan filled with an evil design to deceive, for an example (Acts 5:1-11).

Satan also succeeded at hindering the mighty Apostle Paul in his work (I Thessalonians 2:18).

---

24 In Chapter 16, I discuss particularly how new cart preaching has removed God from American politics and effectively turned our government over to Satan.

When the Apostle Paul encountered opposition that thwarted his plans to visit the Thessalonians (I Thessalonians 2:18), he did not defer to the hindrance as evidence that it was not God's will for him to go. In similar circumstances, most Christians today would say, effectively, "Oh well; I guess it was not God's will." Instead, Paul discerned that somehow the devil had succeeded at hindering his purpose. This apostle exhorted us to wear all the armor of God so we could withstand the wiles of the devil (Ephesians 6:11).

If the Corinthians, who were not ignorant of Satan's devices, were warned to beware lest Satan get an advantage among them (II Corinthians 2:11), consider what advantage the devil has in churches that are ignorant of his devices? Paul understood that Satan is active in the world today (Revelation 2:13), and that he is able to harass believers and hinder their work. Most new cart Christians are oblivious to spiritual warfare, and Satan likes it that way.

The fact that evil spirits are active in the world and that they involve themselves in hindering our work for the Lord ought to be obvious to all believers. The Apostle Paul warned us that seducing spirits would be involved in leading believers into false doctrines (I Timothy 4:1-4). The Apostle John knew that evil spirits would attempt to deceive us and warned us to "try the spirits whether they are of God" (I John 4:1).

The Spirit warns us that we "wrestle not against flesh and blood, but against principalities, against powers, against the rulers of the darkness of this world, against spiritual wickedness in high places" (Ephesians 6:12). The verse makes it clear that the principalities and powers we wrestle against are not of the flesh and blood variety spoken of in Titus 3:1. The Spirit speaks of "the principalities and powers in heavenly places" (Ephesians 3:10).

We fight this spiritual war with spiritual weapons (II Corinthians 10:4). Paul explains the armor we are to wear (Ephesians 6:13-16a), the weapon we are to wield (Ephesians 6:13b), and the principle tactic of our warfare—intercessory prayer for boldness to preach the gospel with effect (Ephesians 6:19-20).

There is a war going on, and I hope to pull back the veil of the physical and to allow you a peek at the spiritual warfare that rages between the Holy Spirit of Jesus Christ and the unholy spirit of antichrist. We are soldiers engaged in this war. It is important that we understand it.

Jesus created all "principalities and powers" (Colossians 1:16). According to Colossians 1:16, there are both visible and invisible principalities and powers. The visible principalities and powers are the physical, flesh and blood principalities and powers that operate in the earth. The invisible principalities and powers refer to the spirits that operate in the world from their headquarters in heavenly places (Ephesians 3:10). These include the angels of God who operate in the earth under the authority of God whose throne is in what is called the third Heaven (II Corinthians 12:2; Revelation 4-5). These angels minister to those on earth who are the heirs of salvation (Hebrews 1:14). Of course, these spirits work the works of God in the earth. Also there are the spirits who operate in the earth from the second Heaven, under the prince and power of the air (Ephesians 2:2). These are called devils (Matthew 8:16) or seducing spirits (I Timothy 4:1), and they work against the purposes of God in the earth.

God gave the dominion of the earth to man (Genesis 1:26-28) and warned him that if he chose sin, he would die (Genesis 2:17).

Satan desires to usurp God's place over man in the principalities and powers of the earth (Isaiah 14:12-17; Daniel 10:10-20).

Satan succeeded at tempting man into sin thus gaining the power of death over mankind (Genesis 3; Hebrews 2:14). He set out to corrupt mankind and thereby alienate him from God so he could rule on earth as god of this world (II Corinthians 4:4).

He nearly succeeded at corrupting the entire human race, provoking God to destroy all mankind with a flood (Genesis 6:6-7), but Noah found grace in the eyes of the LORD (Genesis 6:8). From Noah, a new generation of humanity began to populate the earth.

Nimrod was a descendant of one of Noah's sons, Ham. He was the first to make himself a king over men, establishing the first kingdom on the earth (Genesis 10:10). He led the people in a revolt against God (Genesis 11:1-9). After God scattered the people at Babel (which became Babylon, in modern day Iraq), they followed the pattern of Nimrod and established kingdoms ruled by men all over the earth. These kingdoms vied against one another for control of the dominion God gave to Adam. Satan pursued control of the earth by corrupting these kingdoms and provoking God to give him power over them.

God established His own nation, the Israelites, and maintained a foothold in the earth through Israel. Satan finally succeeded at corrupting Israel until God destroyed them and turned the dominion over to the Gentiles. At this time, God repeatedly affirmed that it is He Who gives the kingdom (the dominion) to whomever He will (Daniel 4:17, 25, 32). Through the prophet Daniel, God revealed the succession of the dominion from Nebuchadnezzar to the establishment of His Own Son, the last Adam, as the rightful heir of the dominion (Daniel 2-12).

Nebuchadnezzar was the first heathen king to receive the dominion after God destroyed Israel and Judah. God referred to Nebuchadnezzar as His servant. Soon after, Satan went to work corrupting Babylon and finally succeeded (Daniel 5).

God gave the dominion to another of His servants named Cyrus the Persian. Daniel tells us about the spiritual warfare that was going on during this time as the prince of Persia attempted to bring the dominion under the power of Satan (Daniel 10).

After Satan succeeded at corrupting Persia, God turned the dominion over to Alexander's Greece (Daniel 8). God does not refer to Alexander as His servant. This king was broken quickly and his kingdom divided.

Then came the fourth kingdom (Daniel 7). By this time Satan had gained power over all the kingdoms of the world (Luke 4:5-8).

But God sent His own Son, Jesus Christ, into the world to break the power of Satan over man and cast him out (John 12:31).

In order to break Satan's hold on mankind, Jesus had to take from Satan the power of death (Hebrews 2:14). He did this by paying the wages of sin, which is death (Romans 6:23). Because Jesus was without sin (Hebrews 4:15), death could not hold Him (I Corinthians 15:55-56). He died not for His own sins but for the sins of the world (I John 2:1-2). Because sin had no power over Him, He had the power to take up His life again (John 10:17-18). By His resurrection, He was declared to be the Son of God *with power* (Romans 1:4).

Jesus, having therefore spoiled all principalities and powers by His cross, was given all power in Heaven and in earth (Colossians 2:15-16; Matthew 28:18-20).

He went into Heaven to receive for Himself a kingdom (Luke 19:12; Acts 1:9; Hebrews 1:3; 8:1), but He put His Spirit into our hearts (Ephesians 3:17; Galatians 4:6) and left us here as His servants to carry on the work of declaring Jesus is LORD, and calling on all men everywhere to repent and believe on Him to be saved from the wrath to come (Romans 10:9-13; Acts 17:30; Luke 24:47-49).

Satan was banished from the earth and operates now as prince of the power of the air, the spirit who now works in the children of disobedience (Ephesians 2:2). He is doing all in his power to reclaim his place in the earth by displacing our place in it. He is using the same tactics he used to corrupt Israel. Before the last apostle died, Satan had already reestablished his "seat" (throne) in the earth at Pergamos (Revelation 2:13). We cannot help but notice that the first thing he introduced in Pergamos was tolerance for what Christ hates (Revelation 2:6, 15). Soon thereafter, he infiltrated the church of Thyatira with a pagan priestess named Jezebel (Revelation 2:18-29).

Nevertheless, the Spirit of Jesus Christ in us is greater than the spirit of antichrist in them (I John 4:4). Indeed, His Spirit in us restrains the spirit of antichrist in this world (II Thessalonians 2:7-8), hindering Satan's efforts to complete Nimrod's dream of creating a one-world government ruled by a satanically inspired man of sin.

Jesus warned us to give no place to the devil (Ephesians 4:27). We have failed, and Satan has taken hold of much of the earth today. Hence there is an ongoing war between the spirit of antichrist in the world (I John 4:3) and the Spirit of Jesus Christ in us. The opposing armies in this war are the children of disobedience on one side (II Thessalonians 1:8), and the children of obedience on the other (Romans 6:17).

The devils that operate on behalf of the spirit of antichrist are strengthened when they are able to seduce those indwelt by the Spirit of Jesus Christ to walk in the flesh (Romans 8:1-5), and thereby grieve the Spirit (Ephesians 4:30-31).

New cart churches are oblivious to all of this. Unknowingly, they strengthen the powers of darkness in this world and limit the Holy One (Psalm 78:41).

Our concern is that most churches today do not have a *soldiers of the Cross* mentality. You would not characterize new cart churches as at war with the world, the flesh, and the devil. Instead, the attitude of new cart ministries suggests they are at peace with the world, the flesh, and, therefore, "by default," with the devil too. The character of the preaching and the overall presentation of the ministry to the world is not one of soldier–ambassadors charging the gates of hell reproving the unfruitful works of darkness. Rather, these churches are more like social clubs than training camps, amusement parks than forward operating bases for spiritual warriors.

Another way to know you are in a new cart church is if that church ministry is under leadership that is not leading the church in spiritual warfare. New cart churches discourage the flow of the Spirit of Jesus Christ into the world through the belly of His disciples (John 7:38-39). They grieve the Spirit of Christ in the earth and unwittingly aid and abet the antichrist spirit.

Chapter Eleven

The
Fruit of the Spirit

Question Five: *Does the church manifest the fruit of the Spirit of Christ?*

THE FRUIT OF THE SPIRIT is *love, joy, peace, longsuffering, gentleness, goodness, faith, meekness,* and *temperance* (Galatians 5:22-23). The Apostle Paul exhorted the believers in Ephesus to endeavor to keep "the unity of the Spirit in the bond of peace" (Ephesians 4:3). He reproved the Corinthian church for their divisions (I Corinthians 3:1-8). Churches that are not characterized by the fruit of the Spirit, or that are characterized by quarrelsome divisions, have come under the control and influence of another spirit. These churches are not manifesting the Spirit of Christ.

Unfortunately, the world has corrupted the meaning of almost every one of the words the Bible uses to describe the fruit of the Holy Spirit. For example, love is understood as human affection that motivates someone to be sensitive to the feelings of others. That's OK, so far as it goes, but according to the wisdom of the world it is insensitive, and therefore unloving to rebuke someone. Yet Jesus said, "As many as I love, I rebuke and chasten" (Revelation 3:19).

Because many Christians have accepted the world's corruption of the concept of love, they are confused about how to rightly identify a church that is guided by the Spirit of God. They are likely to think a church that preaches against homosexuality and abortion, or that speaks against the sins of our nation, is mean-spirited, unkind, and ungenerous. Instead, they are deceived into following churches that are guided by the spirit of this world (Ephesians 2:2).

We could fill several pages illustrating how the world has corrupted every quality identified as the fruit of the Spirit. The following summary, however, will give you the idea.

The world has reduced joy to feeling happy, peace to the absence of struggle, longsuffering to tolerance, gentleness to tenderness, goodness to whatever makes one feel good about themselves, faith to mere belief, meekness to passivity, and temperance to anything goes in moderation. There may be some semblance of truth in some of these, but they represent a very shallow and superficial understanding of these qualities.

God desires us to be happy (Psalm 128:2). But He warns us against those who take "pleasure in unrighteousness" (II Thessalonians 2:12). Besides, happiness is only one aspect of joy; and the world has reduced it to superficial elation. True joy and happiness go much deeper and sustain us even in times of great trials (James 1:2).

Longsuffering certainly includes tolerance, but tolerance toward evil leads to an accommodation of evil, and finally to a capitulation to it. Invariably, tolerance of evil results in intolerance toward the righteous (Proverbs 29:27). Consider the Spirit of Jesus on the matter of being tolerant of false teaching: "But this thou hast, that thou hatest the deeds of the Nicolaitans, which I also hate" (Revelation 2:6). The Spirit of Jesus Christ is contrary to the spirit of the new cart church today.

We are exhorted to "Be gentle unto all men" (II Timothy 2:24). Gentleness requires us to maintain control of our strength when provoked. To be mindful of the possibility our strength might hurt another is always good, but if we hold back our strength from the execution of judgment we strengthen evil (Jeremiah 48:10; Ecclesiastes 8:11).

Regarding faith, consider that the devils believe and tremble (James 2:18-19), but they don't exercise faith. Clearly, faith is more than merely believing; it involves a surrender to what is believed.

Meekness is grossly misunderstood by the world. Much of what is said concerning gentleness might also be said concerning meekness. Moses illustrates the truth that to be meek is not to be passive. He was called the meekest man in his generation, but he was certainly not a pacifist (Exodus 32:19).

As for temperance, the idea that anything is acceptable if done in moderation is seen as patently absurd the moment we apply it to murder, rape, or to any behavior God has declared ungodly.

But the above is only a cursory look at the question. I challenge you to study the Scripture's use of these words. Compare what you learn to how the world views these things and you will see that the world has corrupted these words. Any Christian understanding them from the world's point of view will be led away from a church that is truly guided by the Holy Spirit into a church that is under the influence of another spirit. Perhaps now you understand why Satan works so hard to pervert our understanding of these things and why it is so important to study to show yourself approved unto God (II Timothy 2:15).

Chapter Twelve

The Manifestation of the Spirit

Question Six: *Does the Spirit of Christ manifest in the assembly?*

WHAT GIVES EVIDENCE THAT GOD is in a congregation? In I Corinthians 14:24-25, the Spirit says, "But if all prophesy, and there come in one that believeth not, or one unlearned, he is convinced of all, he is judged of all: and thus are the secrets of his heart made manifest; and so falling down on his face he will worship God, and report that God is in you of a truth." Prophesying does not mean telling the future. It means to declare God's Words to others. When the Word of God is taught and preached, the Spirit uses the light of God's Word to expose the sins of the hearts of everyone present. This is how we can know that God is in this people, and in this place.

The Bible also says the Spirit is manifested in a church by the gifts of the Spirit: "But the manifestation of the Spirit is given to every man to profit withal" (I Corinthians 12:7). To *profit withal* means to benefit all present.

Word of wisdom, word of knowledge, faith, healing, miracles, prophecy, discerning of spirits, divers kinds of tongues, and the interpretation of tongues are named in I Corinthians 12:8-10.

As members interact with one another, and while the Word of God is being ministered to the congregation, the Spirit of Christ ministers to the people.

The Spirit might impart a special and needed insight of wisdom or knowledge. One member who is disheartened might receive from the Spirit a special ministration of faith to encourage him or her. Sometimes the Spirit quickens members to pray in faith over another member's sickness and the Spirit ministers healing through them.

Then there are miracles. The word that is translated miracles refers to an open demonstration of the power of God to affect some divine work. One example might be when the believers are gathered for assembly and suddenly a great storm falls upon the city and someone in the congregation is stirred by the Spirit to call on God and to command the storm to pass over, and it does.

One believer might be moved by the Spirit to prophesy, which in this case means to declare the Word of God to a particular issue or question, or even to declare what God intends to do in a certain situation.

When a believer is troubled by sensitivity to a false or foul spirit that has entered the group, he or she will be manifesting the Spirit by the gift of discerning of spirits.

All of these manifestations are subject to being tried by the Word of God (I John 4:1) and by those whose senses are sharpened by it to discern between good and evil (Hebrews 5:14). Nevertheless, any church guided and controlled by the Spirit of God will experience these manifestations.

Finally, we come to the issue of tongues and the interpretation of tongues. We notice that the Apostle Paul dedicated one entire chapter to address this gift (I Corinthians 14). It has been a controversial matter in the churches for millennia. Therefore, we will set aside special consideration for this gift in the next chapter.

Chapter Thirteen

Obeying the
Holy Spirit

Question Seven: *Does the congregation obey the Scripture in the matter of the sign gift of tongues?*

W HAT ABOUT THE SIGN gift of tongues? In the previous chapter, we discussed the truth that the Holy Ghost manifests in the congregation through conviction upon the conscience of all present under the preaching of the Word of God (I Corinthians 14:20-24). We also discussed the truth that a church manifesting the Spirit will be generally characterized by the fruit of the Spirit (Galatians 5:21-22) and will experience the manifestation of the Spirit by spiritual gifts (I Corinthians 12). In this chapter, we will look especially at the sign gift of tongues.

Like all the gifts named in I Corinthians 12, the gift of tongues is a manifestation of the Spirit (I Corinthians 12:7). However, the behavior of the Corinthians that is described in I Corinthians 14:7-13 can be characterized in only one way—confusion. God is not the author of confusion (I Corinthians 14:33). It is obvious that the activity Paul corrects in I Corinthians 14 was not something the Spirit of God was manifesting; it was something else.

We notice that the gift of tongues is the only one for which God gave instructions governing its expression. These instructions cannot be intended to control how the Spirit of God chooses to manifest Himself by this gift. Clearly, the Spirit through Paul was giving instructions that would allow believers to try the spirits at work in these congregations to see if they are of God (I John 4:1).

The instructions are very clear, one at a time, no more than three, and there must be an interpreter (I Corinthians 14:27-28).

Additionally, the command to "Let your women keep silence in the churches: for it is not permitted unto them to speak" (I Corinthians 14:34), must be understood in its context. Since women are instructed to be teachers of good things, and to teach the younger women to love their husbands (Titus 2:3-4), and because both men and women are commanded to be witnesses of the gospel, we do not understand this verse to mean women cannot teach, or witness. In the immediate context of the command, we are talking about speaking in tongues and prophesying (specifically in the congregation of the Lord's people) (I Corinthians 14:26).

We know that if any of these rules are violated, whatever manifested was not the Spirit of the Lord, but some other spirit.

Furthermore, we learn from the Apostle Paul that this particular gift is a sign to the unbelieving Jew (I Corinthians 14:21-25). Signs were established in the Scripture to mark the fulfillment of prophetic events. In I Corinthians 14:21, Paul quotes Isaiah 28:11-12. He explained that tongues signaled the fulfillment of one of Isaiah's prophecies concerning Israel.

Isaiah 28:11-12 says, "For with stammering lips and another tongue will he speak to this people. To whom He said, This is the rest wherewith ye may cause the weary to rest; and this is the refreshing: yet they would not hear." The prophecy was to *this people,* and the context of Isaiah 28 makes it clear that the people to whom he was speaking was Israel. Also, the prophecy is addressed particularly to those in Israel who *would not hear.*

We know that Paul, a Jew, heard and received the promised rest (Hebrews 4:1-11), as did many other Jews, 3,000 on Pentecost alone (Acts 2:41). But this prophecy was specifically addressed to the

Jews who would fulfill the prediction referred to in Hebrews 3:11 "So I sware in my wrath, They shall not enter into my rest." In other words, according to the Spirit of God, the gift of tongues was a sign not to the believing Jew, but to the Jews who did not believe.

As with all signs, they are no longer looked for once they have been fulfilled. For example, Isaiah 7:14 speaks of the sign of the virgin birth. It has been fulfilled; we no longer look for this sign to occur. The Spirit of God formally declared the fulfillment of the prophecy of Isaiah in Acts 28:28. The sign gift of tongues had been presented, indicating the gospel that ministers the refreshing and the rest God had promised them had come, but the Jews, as a nation, rejected it. Therefore, God cut off the unbelieving Jew and grafted in the believing Gentile (Romans 10-11).[25]

Understanding that the prophecy regarding tongues is addressed to the Jews who would not believe explains something Paul said by the Spirit in I Corinthians 14:21-25 that is otherwise inexplicable. In verse 22, Paul says tongues are for a sign, not to them that believe, but to them that believe not. Does this mean He intended the sign gift of tongues as a way to reach "sinners of the Gentiles" (Galatians 2:15)? No. The Spirit is saying that the sign gift of tongues was a sign to the Jews who would refuse to believe. It was not a sign to *unbelieving* Gentiles. The unlearned and unbelieving (always a reference to the ignorant Gentiles) would not understand tongues because they would not recognize it as a *sign*. However, the Jews, who were familiar with Isaiah 28:11-12, would be in a position to understand exactly what this meant.

Often I am asked if the gift of tongues was a sign gift to the Jews who would reject Jesus as Messiah, why did the Spirit manifest this gift through Gentiles (Acts 10). In Acts 15, Peter was able to use

---

25 During these last days (Hebrews 1:1) Jesus is walking in the midst of the churches in the earth (Revelation 2:1), to whom He gave the keys of the kingdom (Matthew 16:17-18). The refreshing promised to Israel as a nation (Acts 3:19; Isaiah 28:11-12) was the restoration of her kingdom. She rejected it, and so during this dispensation it is now extended to any Gentile nation receiving the gospel and bringing forth the fruit of the kingdom (Matthew 21:43).

the manifestation of tongues among the Gentiles in the house of Cornelius as a sign to the Jews that the refreshing it signified had been extended to the Gentiles as well as to the Jews.

The above might be a bit meaty for some reading this. I encourage you to study the Scriptures to show yourself approved unto God, and if the above study is deeper than you are accustomed to going in the Word, consider Hebrews 5:13-14. Also ask yourself whether you are in a church where the teachers are fulfilling their purpose to feed the flock of God (Acts 20:28) so that you will "henceforth be no more children, tossed to and fro, and carried about with every wind of doctrine, by the sleight of men, and cunning craftiness, whereby they lie in wait to deceive" (Ephesians 4:14).

Additionally, it's important to understand that the reason God allows heresies (doctrinal errors) to run through a fellowship is to distinguish those whom God has approved for ministry. Read I Corinthians 11:19: "For there must needs be heresies among you, that they which are approved may be manifest among you." Think about it! The Spirit, by Paul, explained that heresies are necessary in order that those who are approved students of the Word will be made manifest. Therefore every preacher is exhorted to heed what Paul told Timothy: "Study to shew thyself approved unto God, a workman that needeth not to be ashamed, rightly dividing the word of truth" (II Timothy 2:15).

New cart preachers do not study to show themselves approved unto God; they study to gain the approval of men.

One way to know whether the Spirit of God guides a church is whether the church is manifesting spiritual gifts obediently. Something is wrong if a church shows no manifestation of the Spirit. Perhaps they are ignorant of spiritual gifts (I Corinthians 12:1), or temporarily out of fellowship with God. But something is very seriously wrong when a church refuses to submit to the authority of the Spirit of God as revealed by the Apostle Paul regarding the sign gift of tongues. That church is not only grieving the Spirit, but is following another spirit altogether.

Chapter Fourteen

Worshiping in Spirit

Question Seven: *Does the church worship in spirit?*

JESUS SAID TO THE Samaritan woman, "But the hour cometh, and now is, when the true worshipers shall worship the Father **in spirit** and in truth: for the Father seeketh such to worship Him" (John 4:23–emphasis added).

This Samaritan woman considered herself to be a believer. She identified with the congregation of Israel, claiming Jacob as her father (John 4:11). Yet Jesus told her that she did not know what she worshiped (John 4:22). How can this be?

The Jews, especially the Pharisees, looked upon the Samaritans as spiritual mongrels. Of course, this plays into the stereotype of Pharisees as hypocritical, self-righteous bigots. So before I go any further, I need to address the characteristic disdain every new cart Christian has for the Pharisees because this is a major point of tension between new cart and old path Christians.

Jewish believers were divided into two major sects: the Pharisees and the Sadducees. The Pharisees believed the Scriptures were divinely inspired, that is, written by God through men. Taking

Scriptures literally, they believed in angels and in the resurrection of the dead. Additionally, the Pharisees were very strict in their observance of the Law of Moses. The Sadducees interpreted the Scriptures loosely, and accepted only the writings of Moses as authoritative. Sadducees denied the existence of angels and the resurrection of the dead (Matthew 22:23; Acts 23:8). By comparison to today, the Pharisees were the conservatives and the Sadducees were the liberals.

Jesus affirmed both the resurrection and belief in angels. In fact, His basic teachings lined up closely with that of the Pharisees. Most agree that Peter, his brother Andrew, James, and John were all Pharisees. In fact, with the possible exception of Levi, who was a Publican (Luke 5:27), and Simon, who was a Zealot (Luke 6:15), it is generally agreed that all the early disciples were of the sect called the Pharisees. Christ's disciples expressed concern when it appeared Jesus might alienate Himself from this sect (Matthew 12:38), suggesting they considered it a negative thing, which further suggests they had sympathy with that sect. In fact the Pharisees believed all the fundamentals of the Jewish faith that Jesus taught, with one exception—His claim to be the Messiah.

Notice that when Jesus looked for some human standard to help His disciples understand His high call to personal righteousness, He chose the high standard set by the Pharisees (Matthew 5:20). By most accounts, Paul was the greatest of all the apostles, and in his day all believers would consider it a proper boast for Paul to say, "Circumcised the eighth day, of the stock of Israel, of the tribe of Benjamin, an Hebrew of the Hebrews; as touching the law, a Pharisee" (Philippians 3:5).

Jesus rebuked the Pharisees more harshly than anyone else (Matthew 23:13-36). So perhaps it surprises you to discover that He drew virtually all of His early disciples from among the Pharisees, and that His doctrinal orientation was closely aligned with that sect. Remember, Jesus said, "As many as I love, I rebuke and chasten" (Revelation 3:19). The liberal Sadducees were hardly worth His attention or mention.

Of course, we all should avoid the self-righteous attitudes typical of the Pharisees (Luke 18:11). But let's be careful we don't become equally self-righteous in our scorn of them.

The reason virtually all Jews regarded the Samaritans as spiritual mongrels was because they were descendants of the Israelites who were exiled by the king of Assyria in 721 BC and mingled with the Gentile nations. They had diluted the true Jewish faith and incorporated into their thinking many of the pagan beliefs they picked up from the heathen. Nevertheless, the Samaritans thought they worshiped the same God as their Jewish ancestors.

At Jacob's well, Jesus encountered one of these Samaritans. She believed the only real difference between them was that her fathers worshiped in Mt. Gerizim, while the rest of the Jews worshiped in Jerusalem. But the truth is that the Samaritans had become so confused in their thinking about God, they really did not know what they worshiped. Her forefathers developed an ecumenical religion in which they assumed everyone worshiped the same God, only by different names, with different methods, and in different places. However, Jesus said the Samaritans did not know what they worshiped.[26] Her problem was not a question of where she chose to worship. It was a question of what she was worshiping. What we worship is always a concern. But regarding her specific question, Jesus made it clear that in the New Testament era, *where* was not going to be an issue but *how* would be the issue. Jesus said the Father wanted His people to worship Him in spirit and in truth.

So, what does it mean to worship *in spirit*?

God rejects any form of worship that draws our spirit into the flesh. That is because He desires that we worship Him in spirit, not in flesh.

In the Bible, the word *flesh* is used to speak of the sin nature that we inherited from Adam (Romans 5:11-12). When Adam sinned the

---

26 The word *ye* is plural. It identifies a group and the individuals in it. He said, "Ye worship ye know not what" (John 4:22). This means He was not saying merely that this particular woman did not know what she worshiped. He was saying she and her people, the Samaritans, did not know what they worshiped.

law of sin took up permanent residence in the members of his body (Romans 7:23). This condition is passed to us at birth (Romans 5:12), so that every child is born under the sentence of death (Romans 6:23). It corrupted our nature so that in our flesh there is no good thing (Romans 7:18).

When we are born again (John 3:3-7; I Peter 1:23), the Spirit of God takes up residence in our heart (Galatians 4:6), and we are *circumcised,* that is, the foreskin of our *flesh* is cut away from our *heart.* Physical circumcision (Genesis 17:11; Ephesians 2:11) is a picture of spiritual circumcision (Colossians 2:11; Romans 2:29).

Once the flesh is cut away from our heart, God places His Law in our inward parts and writes it upon our heart (Jeremiah 31:33).

With the Law of God in our heart and the law of sin in our members, we are in a constant strife between the Spirit Who resides in our heart and the sin that resides in our flesh (Galatians 5:17).

Paul talked about worshiping God in the spirit: Philippians 3:3, "For we are the circumcision, which worship God in the spirit, and rejoice in Christ Jesus, and have no confidence in the flesh."

Our human spirit communes with God's Holy Spirit (Romans 8:16). We are called upon to spiritually walk not after the flesh, but after the Spirit (Romans 8:1-9). God would have us worship Him in communion with His Holy Spirit and not in communion with unholy flesh. We can do this because we have been circumcised in our heart (Romans 2:29).

So, when we receive Christ Jesus as LORD and He puts His Spirit into our hearts we are circumcised. The foreskin of the flesh is cut away from our heart and our spirit is set free from its former bondage to the motions of sins in the flesh (Romans 7:5).

Because we have been circumcised in our heart, our spirit is invited to come boldly before the Throne of Grace to petition the Almighty for mercy to find grace to help in time of need (Hebrews 4:16). We enter His presence when our spirit submits to and communes with the Holy Spirit in prayer (Ephesians 6:18).

Worshiping our heavenly Father in the spirit is in contrast with worshiping Him in the flesh. Only when we worship in spirit can our worship be acceptable to God.

The truth that genuine worship must not be fleshly does not mean it is without the body. Paul, by the Spirit, calls upon all believers to present their body a living sacrifice, holy, acceptable unto God as their reasonable service (Romans 12:1). This means surrendering our body to His use. Indeed, the Holy Ghost claims the body of believers as His Temple, the place on earth where the Holy Spirit dwells (I Corinthians 6:19). In this way, the believer's body is an earthen vessel containing the treasure of God (II Corinthians 4:7). Paul was called a "chosen vessel" (Acts 9:15). The vessel must be sanctified for His use (II Timothy 2:21).

Therefore we must cleanse ourselves of all filthiness of the flesh and spirit and perfect holiness in the fear of God (II Corinthians 7:1). This will allow His Spirit to fill the body (Ephesians 5:18). To worship God in spirit we must submit our own spirit to the embrace of the Holy Spirit. It is in that sweet, holy communion in which His Spirit bears witness with ours that we are children of the heavenly Father, and sheds abroad in our hearts His great love that we can experience worshiping God in spirit (Ephesians 5:18; II Corinthians 13:14; Romans 8:16; 5:5).

Practically speaking, this is how it's done.

Our spirit functions through our mind. For example, we are to be renewed in the spirit of our mind (Ephesians 4:23). Our spirit acts with our mind in a manner that is similar to how our soul acts with our body. This is the reason that when we look on a woman to lust after her in our heart, we have, spiritually, committed adultery with her (Matthew 5:28). So our spirit acts by our mind to frame thoughts in our heart that are actions done in the presence of Christ, who by the Spirit of God dwells in our hearts by faith (Ephesians 3:17; Romans 8:9-11).

We are commanded to bring "every thought into the obedience of Christ" (II Corinthians 10:5). When we mind (set our thoughts upon) the things of the Spirit, we walk after the Spirit. When we mind the things of the flesh, we walk after the flesh (Romans 8:5). We cannot worship in spirit when we are minding the flesh.

God repeatedly commands us to be set apart from the world (I John 2:15-16; Romans 12:1-2; II Corinthians 6:17, to cite a few of hundreds). We are called upon to hate this life (Luke 8:14; 14:26; 21:34; II Timothy 2:4), to set our affection on things above and not on things of this earth (Colossians 3:2), and to relish no savor for the things of men (Matthew 16:23). A *worldling* is a Christian whose affections are set on the things of this world, and whose attention is focused on the things of this life. Such Christians are not following the Holy Spirit no matter how spiritual they might otherwise appear to be. They are of another spirit.

Evidence that a congregation is patterning their worship after the flesh is that their worship will be world–friendly. It will appeal to worldlings and flesh-minding Christians. It also appeals to the lost, but not in a good way. It will strengthen the hold that their fleshly appetites already have upon their spirit, and tends to defile the sweet graces of the gospel with vile perversities of the flesh.

It is usually seen in the music because music involves the emotional expression of our spirit and soul through our body. If our spirit is filthy with sinful appetites of the flesh, our worship will also be filthy (II Corinthians 7:1). It's very basic. If a believer is minding the things of the flesh he will naturally use fleshly forms of music in worship. This is offensive to God. To take the forms of music that have originated among the children of disobedience (Ephesians 2:1-2), or that are clearly identifiable with the children of disobedience, is offensive to our Holy God and grieves His Holy Spirit. (Keep in mind that the word *holy* means to be separated from the world and identified with God.)

Whatever is presented in worship that is identifiable with the spirit of rebellion working in the children of disobedience must be as offensive to God as a man walking into a Jewish Synagogue wearing a Nazi swastika would be offensive to the Jews there.

A seducing spirit will surely attempt to neutralize this very poignant point in the mind of some reading this by suggesting the idea that Christians have used worldly music for many centuries. The truth is that before rock-n-roll was introduced, popular forms of music in our Christianized culture did not generally qualify as worldly. Something is not *worldly* merely because it occurs in the world.

Worldliness is defined in I John 2:15 as appealing to the lust of the eyes, the lust of the flesh, and the pride of life. To understand what appeals to our lusts read Galatians 5:16-20. Most pre-rock-n-roll popular music in America grew out of forms originating among God's people. Many of the popular songs of the early fifties were gospel songs. By contrast, rock-n-roll originated with the children of disobedience. It is by design *worldly.*

Mature Christians who exercised themselves in the use of the Scripture so as to sharpen their senses to discern good and evil (Hebrews 5:14) recognized it immediately as the music of rebellion. Of course, they were ridiculed and scorned and ignored, but it was only a few generations later that millions of our children were led into the occult by their rock-n-roll heroes.[27]

Another important point to take from the necessity that we worship God in spirit is that genuine worship is never without the mind fully engaged, fully aware. Any form of worship that encourages one to suspend active engagement of their rational mind during worship is not the sort of worship that God wants. You cannot truly worship in spirit without the understanding being engaged (I Corinthians 14:15).

Any church that uses fleshly forms in worship or engages in worship that separates your understanding from your behavior is not the sort of worship that God will accept. I include it in the category

---

27 The most thorough and well-documented expose of the relationship between rock-n-roll and the occult that I have come across is <u>Rock-n-Roll Sorcerers of the New Age Revolution,</u> produced by *Fight the Good Fight Ministries,* narrated by Pastor Joe Schimmel. http://www.goodfight.org/store/resources_main_video. html (1/30/14)

of new cart worship. Many doing this truly believe they are doing it for the Lord. Because many of these groups attract large crowds of worldlings and flesh-minding believers they think they are blessed by God and successfully reaching the world for Christ. But they mind the things of the flesh (Romans 8:5), and they savor the things that are of men and not of God (Matthew 16:23). The truth is they are not conquering the world for Christ; instead they are unwittingly delivering the churches into the power of darkness.

Chapter Fifteen

Worshiping in Truth

Question Nine: *Does the church worship in truth?*

JESUS SAID, "BUT THE hour cometh, and now is, when the true worshipers shall worship the Father in spirit and **in truth**: for the Father seeketh such to worship Him" (John 4:23–emphasis added).

Not only did Jesus say true worshipers must worship in spirit, but also *in truth*. I have already mentioned the importance of doctrine and the fact that any church that diminishes its importance betrays it is under the influence of a spirit different from the One Who inspired the Scriptures.

Many think the only thing that matters is the sincerity of their heart, and that the proof of their sincerity is how they feel about what they do. Typically, they do not test their sincerity by the objective standard of whether or not they are willing to obey God's Word in a matter. Instead, they use a subjective standard. They judge their own motives to be sincere because when they reflect on their heart they are not aware of any ill feeling toward God, or of any intention to rebel against Him.

I've heard Christians say, in effect, "The Bible might say this or that, but I know in my heart that I am sincere, and that's really what matters." These Christians have subordinated the objective testimony of the Word of God to their own heart. That is very dangerous since the "heart is deceitful and desperately wicked" (Jeremiah 17:9).

Would you regard a Christian truly sincere who disregards the clear teaching of the Bible on a topic? How can any Christian who calls Jesus LORD call that *sincerity*?

Whether we are sincere cannot be determined only by our personal opinions or feelings on a subject. We must "try the spirits" to see if "they are of God" (I John 4:1). Truth is the standard that God has set. The Holy Spirit of God guides us to truth (John 16:13). Jesus declared, "Thy word is truth" (John 17:17). Any spirit unwilling to submit to the truth of God's Word, or that convinces you to make such judgments about your sincerity independent of the "scripture of truth" (Daniel 10:21), is a seducing spirit.

Public or congregational worship involves forms. All worship is going to be expressed in some form or another. The form of worship (that is, the way it is publicly expressed,) is usually shaped by the spirit of the worshipers.

Most new cart Christians I've talked to seem to think the Spirit is decrying the "form of godliness" in II Timothy 3:5, "Having a form of godliness, but denying the power thereof: from such turn away." A form of godliness is a good thing. The problem was that they had a proper form but denied the power of it.

Notice the language, "denying the power *thereof.*" The power is directly connected to the form. These believers are to be avoided because they look right, but they are not right. They have the appearance of authentic worship, but they are devoid of the anointing of the Holy Ghost that gives a godly form any true significance.

This does not mean I support the use of forms described for the Old Testament priesthood, or the use of various ancient pagan forms of worship, such as we find in the Catholic traditions.

Pagan forms incorporated into the worship of the Catholic Church do not arise out of godliness; they are not expressions of worshiping in spirit and in truth because the Bible expressly forbids the use of images in worship (Exodus 20:4-5[28]; I Thessalonians 1:9).

The New Testament priesthood is nowhere instructed to wear the peculiar garments of the Aaronic priesthood for the simple reason that we are not inducted into that priesthood. The New Testament believer (II Corinthians 3:6; Hebrews 9:15) is inducted into a priesthood that is under the High Priest of our profession, Christ Jesus, namely, the Melchisedec priesthood (Hebrews 5:6; Hebrews 3:1; I Peter 2:5; Revelation 1:5-6).

God cares about how we worship Him. In the Old Testament era, it was important that believers gathered for public worship in Jerusalem. That was the controversial issue the woman at the well raised with Jesus (John 4:23). He explained that the day would come when it would not matter where you worshiped, but what would matter is how you worship. He told her that God seeks worshipers to worship Him in spirit and in truth.

The New Testament does not formalize any doctrine on what forms we should use in our worship. Yet the Bible does offer some insight into the forms of worship the Spirit has blessed in His congregation.

Most of the early churches followed the pattern of the synagogue. This included a *bishop* (teaching leader of the congregation–I Timothy 3:1-6; I Peter 5:2; Acts 20:28) speaking to the congregation from a pulpit made of wood (Nehemiah 8:4), opening the Scriptures, reading them, and giving the sense of them. This included preaching, which involved reproving, rebuking, and exhorting the congregation from the Scriptures (II Timothy 4:2).

---

28 The Scripture instructs us very specifically not to bow down before statues. The rationalization that these are being used as *aids to worship* or that the worshiper is conscious that they are not worshiping the image but rather what it represents is beside the point. Animists say the same thing, that is, that they worship the spirit in the tree, and likewise Hindu worshipers say they don't worship the image, but what it represents. The fact is God's Spirit has said that believers using such images in worship are unwittingly worshiping devils (I Corinthians 10:20).

Additionally, the worship of the early church involved the singing of psalms, hymns, and spiritual songs (Colossians 3:16). A music leader directing the music is suggested in the fact that the Psalms were committed to the "Chief Musician" (Psalm 4:0; 5:0; 6:0).

Prayers were made in the congregation with the lifting up of hands in worship (I Timothy 2:8; Lamentations 3:41), or in praise. Indeed, Jesus expects His Father's House to be a house of prayer (Isaiah 56:78; Matthew 21:13; I Timothy 3:15).

The giving and receiving of offerings to the Lord for His work was a part of congregational worship in the early church (I Corinthians 16:1; Malachi 3:9-11; I Corinthians 9:11-14).

The Corinthians had some peculiar forms that most churches do not follow today (I Corinthians 14:26-31). This is mostly owing to the problems the Corinthians had in their worship that required so much correction. At the bottom line, so long as the form does not contradict any biblical truth, and is done in the spirit, it will be acceptable to our heavenly Father.

Even though it is true that a church may employ all of these forms of godliness and yet deny *the power thereof,* it would seem that any church worship that is guided by the Holy Spirit would tend toward expressing that worship through similar forms.

The patterns of worship that originated with the congregation of the Lord and that were used in the synagogues were rooted in biblical faith. Later, some of the Gentile churches began adopting forms that had originated in their former heathen religions. Thyatira followed in this path and brought serious error into the church (Revelation 2:18-23).

Some forms of worship practiced in churches today originated in heathen worship and are not appropriate for those who desire to worship in spirit and in truth. Likewise, some forms of worship in churches today originated in the world of unbelievers, among the children of disobedience, and so have no place in worship that is supposed to be in spirit and in truth.

For example, some churches hope to attract worshipers by purposely creating a bar room, or nightclub atmosphere. But what they attract are Christian worldlings in addition to non-Christians, who love darkness more than light (John 3:18-21). In their vanity, these churches imagine they are reaching these people. However, lovers of darkness do not come to the light. The gospel takes root only in an honest and good heart (Luke 8:15). Using the methods Satan employs to hold his own in darkness will never be effective to deliver them from it. Like David, these new cart churches attempt to use the methods of the *Philistines,* but they are bringing death into their churches.

One more word regarding forms of worship is needed. We should be charitable in our attitudes toward brothers in Christ who have strayed into unbiblical forms of worship ignorantly. This might surprise you, since I've spent considerable time warning against unbiblical, and especially against worldly, forms of worship. I don't mean we should approve of their errors, but I do mean we should have the same spirit that Hezekiah, the king of Judah, had during the revival of the house of God that took place under his leadership in the early years of his reign (II Chronicles 29:1-11).

About 250 years before Hezekiah, there had been a great split in the congregation of Israel (I Kings 12). The faction that departed from Judah followed Jeroboam in his rebellion against the Lord. Jeroboam did not want the people to go to Jerusalem to worship, fearing if they did their heart would turn back to Judah's king, Rehoboam (I Kings 12:25-32). Therefore, he set up two golden calves and called on the people to worship them. Furthermore, he created his own priesthood and founded a false religion that was a mixture of Judaism with Baalism.

This opened the door for a later king of Israel, named Ahab, to marry a priestess of Baal, Jezebel, who taught Baalism throughout Israel (I Kings 17-18). By the time Hezekiah became king of Judah, Israel had forgotten the right way of the Lord.

When Hezekiah restored the house of God in Jerusalem (II Chronicles 29:1-11), a revival broke out among the people. He sent letters to invite those of the rebellious faction to come and join them in worship (II Chronicles 30:1).

The rebellious Israelites laughed it off but some did attend the revival (II Chronicles 30:10-12). However, they had forgotten the way of the LORD and did not understand the importance of worshiping the LORD according to truth. They did "eat the Passover otherwise than it was written" (II Chronicles 30:18).

Hezekiah did not rebuke them in this case. He did not chastise them nor did he separate them from the revival. Instead, he prayed for them: "But Hezekiah prayed for them, saying, The good LORD pardon every one that prepareth his heart to seek God, the LORD God of his fathers, though he be not cleansed according to the purification of the sanctuary. And the LORD hearkened to Hezekiah, and healed the people" (II Chronicles 30:18-20).

Of course, this should not be taken to suggest it did not matter to God that the people offended in eating the Passover otherwise than it was written. Indeed, a judgment had already begun. But God heard the gracious prayer of the leader of this revival and had mercy upon them for their ignorant offense and healed them.

The point here is that while forms are important, and we should desire to do everything "as it was written," we should not fail to appreciate anyone who "prepareth his heart to seek God." I have learned over the years that if a man prepares his heart to seek God, he will find Him, and the Spirit of truth will guide him to truth. Remember that Jesus taught His disciples to check that spirit that stirs us to oppose any group forming outside of our circle because they "followeth not with us" (Luke 9:49-50).[29]

Jeroboam and the golden calves brings to mind another new cart characteristic that is often found among churches that would

---

29 This becomes a problem today because some attempt to use this Scripture to chastise old path Christians for exercising Romans 16:17, Titus 3:10, and II Corinthians 6:16-17. The Scripture cannot be broken (John 10:35). It's true, he that is "not against us if for us" (Luke 9:50). However, those who teach false doctrine are against us, even if they pretend to be for us.

otherwise look like an old path church. This characteristic is insidious and wicked and it is illustrated by Jeroboam.

God had given 10 of the 12 tribes to Jeroboam (I Kings 11:31-35). One might suppose a sincere hearted leader in such a case would desire to see the congregation reunited. Furthermore, having received this promotion from the LORD, you would expect he would be careful to seek the LORD and lead the people to do the same. Instead, Jeroboam became fearful that the people would return to the king of Judah if they worshiped in Jerusalem (I Kings 12:26-29). Therefore he created two golden calves and set them up as a way to differentiate the worship of his following from those who followed Rehoboam.

Vain church leaders can become jealous over their congregations and foolishly imagine that they own the flock that God gave them. In their foolish jealousy some create issues that are not truly biblical concerns in order to keep people who follow them from following after other leaders they don't like, or have some issue with. They create divisions over traditions of men, and often go so far as to create false doctrines.

Often preachers do this because they are jealous of another man's success. Maybe it's motivated by a fear that their followers will esteem that brother more than them, or even leave them and join the other brother. Or perhaps they hope to attract some of his followers away from him. These wicked, vain men fabricate golden calf issues to use as an excuse to attack the brother, church, school, or other ministry.

Creating these false issues to separate flocks from one another is wicked. It is like Jeroboam's golden calves and any church participating in that behavior is of another spirit.

Our heavenly Father seeks those who will worship Him in spirit and in truth. Seducing spirits teaching doctrines of devils have succeeded at leading new cart Christians into forms of worship that are fleshly and false.

Chapter Sixteen

Christianity Without Christ

Question Ten: *Do they preach Christianity without Christ?*

WILLIAM BOOTH, FOUNDER of the Salvation Army, is famous for saying, "The chief danger that confronts the coming century will be religion without the Holy Ghost, Christianity without Christ, forgiveness without repentance, salvation without regeneration, politics without God, Heaven without hell."[30]

The number one mission of every church and of every Christian in it is to preach the gospel to every creature (Mark 16:15; Matthew 28:18-20; Luke 24:46-48; Acts 1:8). Virtually every Christian church claims that they preach the gospel.

Sadly, as Jesus said to the woman at the well, "ye know not what ye worship," I must say to many evangelical churches and Christians, "Ye know not what ye preach." That is because they have attempted to carry the gospel to sinners in a *new cart*. Using worldly marketing schemes to attract people to their churches, they have built large crowds, but they have failed to build a true church.

30 Booth, William http://www.goodreads.com/author/quotes/151267.William_ Booth (10/8/13)

New cart church evangelism has produced the following: religion without the Holy Ghost, Christianity without Christ, forgiveness without repentance, salvation without regeneration, politics without God, and Heaven without hell.

I will resist the temptation to document all the various ways the new cart church has helped fulfill William Booth's prediction given about 100 years ago. I don't think it's needed. Every true sheep of Christ's pasture reading this who has attended the average contemporary church has seen it, and even if they can't explain it, they know something is missing. Depending on whether they've ever been in a true old path church (Jeremiah 6:16), they might not know exactly what to look for. But those who have had a taste of the Old Fashioned Gospel Hour, or who were carried to church on a bus in the early sixties likely will notice that the preaching today is different. New cart pastors don't preach on hell, they rarely mention repentance, and they don't preach hard against specific sins. Their sermons are more like pep talks to be successful, or counseling talks to rally the family to spend time together, and so on. These things are not evil in and of themselves. And that is just the point. It is not so much a problem with what these preachers are saying as it is with what they are leaving out of their message.

Christianity can be represented to people as a way of life. It can be something someone grows up in and around, without ever coming to know Christ personally. It is possible for preachers to preach sermon after sermon encouraging people to behave according to the precepts of Christianity and yet never help them to actually come to know Christ personally.

It is possible for individuals to call themselves Christian merely because they identify with that religious classification, or because they attend a Christian church, or because they grew up in a home where the parents identified themselves as Christians. And yet it is possible these people have no actual relationship with Jesus Christ. They might even live by many of the principles of Christianity, but if they have not acknowledged Jesus Christ as Lord, and in faith, believed He arose from the grave, called on Him to save them from their sin, and trusted in Him and Him alone to save them from the wrath of God, then they don't know Christ. They have Christianity without Christ.

The preaching of many new cart pastors today leaves people comfortable in the delusion that they are Christians even though there has been no fundamental change in their lives, even though there is no dynamic relationship with Jesus Christ in their lives, even though there is no evidence in the fruit of their lives. Such preachers preach Christianity without Christ.

In the next few chapters we will examine other characteristics of new cart pulpit ministry.

Chapter Seventeen

Forgiveness Without Repentance

Question Eleven: *Do they preach forgiveness without repentance?*

FORGIVENESS IS POSITIVE; REPENTANCE is negative. The spirit influencing the new cart preachers today motivates them to maintain a facade that is positive, engaging, charming, friendly, nice, kind, and so on. Rebuking and reproving seem to them inconsistent with being loving and kind. Besides, when you start hammering on the repentance thing, that's a turn off. And the new cart preachers avoid anything that is a turn off to sinners.

New cart preachers have no problem preaching the remission of sins.[31] A preacher can wax wonderfully eloquent on the mercy of God and His willingness and readiness to forgive and support all of this with hundreds of Bible verses, but if he leaves out repentance, he has told a lie. There is no forgiveness without repentance.

---

31 The word *remission* means to cancel an obligation, to set one free from a debt. Jesus paid the remittance (payment) for our sins (I John 2:1-2; Romans 5:8-9). Most new cart preachers preach remission faithfully. Most cults emphasize repentance to the exclusion of remission, or they preach repentance as a penitence paid by the sinner for remission. It is very important to understand that repentance is not a payment made by the sinner for remission. The blood Jesus shed on Calvary is the only sufficient remittance for sins (Hebrews 9:22; Romans 5:9; Revelation 1:5-6).

Jesus specifically commanded us to preach both repentance and remission (forgiveness) of sins: "Thus it is written, and thus it behoved Christ to suffer, and to rise from the dead the third day: and that repentance and remission of sins should be preached in his name among all nations, beginning at Jerusalem" (Luke 24:46-47).

Most new cart preachers avoid the subject of repentance altogether, but another way they get around this is to redefine repentance so that it is virtually meaningless. A biblical understanding of repentance is offered in Acts 26:20. Paul was giving a testimony of his own ministry and said he preached to all that they should "repent and turn to God, and do works meet for repentance."

In another place, Paul described repentance as follows:

> For godly sorrow worketh repentance to salvation not to be repented of: but the sorrow of the world worketh death. For behold this selfsame thing, that ye sorrowed after a godly sort, what carefulness it wrought in you, yea, what clearing of yourselves, yea, what indignation, yea, what fear, yea, what vehement desire, yea, what zeal, yea, what revenge! In all things ye have approved yourselves to be clear in this matter. (II Corinthians 7:10-11)

The days when sinners would fall on their face before God and cry out for mercy are gone. Today, people receive Christ as Saviour with about as much seriousness as they have when purchasing a candy bar.

Because repentance is so misunderstood, it is necessary to offer additional insight on this matter.

Repentance is not a promise to never sin again. Christians do sin in the flesh (I John 1:7-9; Romans 7:18-20). Neither does it mean that the sinner has merited salvation through penitence. Salvation is not a reward for repentance. Peter described repentance when he said that Jesus was raised from the dead by the Father and sent to bless us by "turning away every one of you from his iniquities" (Acts

3:26).[32] This shows that the point of the gospel is that sinners will be turned from their iniquities. This agrees with Paul's testimony of what Jesus commissioned him to do when he encountered the Lord on the road to Damascus (see Acts 9):

> And I [Paul] said, Who art thou Lord? And he said, I am Jesus whom thou persecutest. But rise, and stand upon thy feet: for I have appeared unto thee for this purpose, to make thee a minister and a witness both of these things which thou hast seen, and of those things in the which I will appear unto thee; delivering thee from the people, and from the Gentiles, unto whom now I send thee, to open their eyes, and to turn them from darkness to light, and from the power of Satan unto God, that they may receive forgiveness of sins, and inheritance among them which are sanctified by faith that is in me. (Acts 26:15-18)

Notice that in order to receive the remission of sins it is necessary that we must have our eyes opened to the truth, to be turned from darkness to light, and from the power of Satan unto God. This is God's desire for all mankind: "Who will have all men to be saved, and to come unto the knowledge of the truth" (I Timothy 2:4). Hence it is God's command to all mankind, "but now [God] commandeth all men every where to repent" (Acts 17:30).

Paul understood that when Jesus commissioned him to "open their eyes, and to turn them from darkness to light, and from the power of Satan unto God" it meant he was to preach repentance. After he shared his testimony with king Agrippa about his calling to ministry,

---

32 This verse does not say that Jesus *repents* us from our iniquities. It says He extends His blessing to us in turning us away from our iniquities. Jesus died on the Cross to redeem us from all our iniquities (Titus 2:14a). He does this that He might "purify to Himself a peculiar people, zealous of good works" (Titus 2:14b). So the Spirit, by the Apostle Paul, calls on all who name the name of Christ to "depart from iniquity" (II Timothy 2:19). Christ's attitude toward those who refuse to turn from their iniquity is made plain in Luke 13:27 and Matthew 7:23.

what he said next offers clear insight into how he understood the Lord's commission:

> Whereupon, O king Agrippa, I was not disobedient unto the heavenly vision: But showed first unto them of Damascus, and at Jerusalem, and throughout all the coasts of Judaea, and then to the Gentiles, that they should repent and turn to God, and do works meet for repentance. (Acts 26:19-20)

The way Paul conducted his ministry makes it clear that he understood Christ intended that he preach repentance, and also that preaching repentance involved calling on sinners to turn to God. In Acts 14:15 he plainly charged the pagan Gentiles to "turn from [their pagan] vanities unto the living God." In I Thessalonians 1:9, Paul reflected with joy on how the Thessalonians "turned to God from idols."[33]

Some are concerned that to say the sinner must turn from his sins to be saved implies that the sinner is saved by acts of personal reformation. We know that the Bible says we are not saved by works, but by grace through faith (Ephesians 2:8-9; Titus 3:5). The Bible also says, "Unto you first God, having raised up his Son Jesus,

33 The word *turn* offers insight into the biblical meaning of repentance. This is clear from Acts 26:15-26 as well as other passages. Sensitive to the great truth that salvation is an act of God in which by grace and through faith alone a man is saved, and not an act of man that is rewarded by God with salvation, some balk at the notion that a sinner must *turn from sin* to be saved. But Paul did not have this difficulty, and neither should we. Neither repentance, nor the action of turning from the power of Satan to God may be construed to be meritorious acts by which a sinner obtains eternal life. First, it is absurd to suggest repentance is a work of righteousness when as a matter of fact repentance is the acknowledgment that righteousness sufficient for salvation is entirely lacking, for not only do we repent of sins, we also repent of our own righteousnesses which are as filthy rags to God (Isaiah 64:6; Romans 10:3; Philippians 3:9). Furthermore, the godly sorrow that works repentance is a sorrow for sins, and being sorry for sins cannot be construed to be a work of righteousness. The Romanist church makes repentance a virtue, and offers forgiveness as a reward for penitence, but the Bible does not. As for *turning to God,* there is no where else the sinner can turn to be saved. Necessarily, therefore, the sinner must turn to God to be saved. *Turning* to God necessarily involves a turning from sin.

sent him to bless you, in turning away every one of you from his iniquities" (Acts 3:26). But there is nothing in this Scripture that talks about "turning over a new leaf," or personal reformation.

Indeed, no sinner can be saved who turns from his sins and then sets out to establish himself as righteous before God. Even our righteousnesses are as filthy rags to God (Isaiah 64:6). Those who attempt to establish their own righteousness have not submitted themselves to the righteousness of God (Romans 10:3). Yea, we are saved by His righteousness: "To declare, I say, at this time his righteousness: that he might be just, and the justifier of him which believeth in Jesus" (Romans 3:26).

As sin was imputed to us by Adam's sin, and passed on to us by Adam's seed (Romans 5:12-14), so the righteousness of the incarnate Word of God (John 1:1,14) is imputed to us by His righteousness, and passed on to us by His Seed (I Peter 1:23; I John 3:9). Being born of Adam, we are birthed into his sin; being born of God, we are birthed into His righteousness.

The miracle of the new birth is ours when we believe on Him. Jesus explained that lovers of darkness will not believe on him (John 3:19). Hence, it is necessary that the sinner turn from darkness to light in order to be saved (Acts 26:18).

Turning from our iniquities does not mean we have committed to God that we will never again sin. Any Christian who says he has no sin deceives himself, and betrays that he has not the truth in him (I John 1:8). And yet it should be obvious that turning to God for forgiveness of our sins necessarily involves turning away from iniquity, for when a sinner turns to God, his iniquity is purged. Clearly, that godly sorrow that the Bible says *works repentance unto salvation,* moves the heart to yearn for forgiveness of sins, and that is turning from iniquity.

"But," say some, "the Bible plainly teaches sinners are saved by grace through faith" (Ephesians 2:8-10; Romans 3:28; 5:1; Galatians 2:16; 3:11, 24). To which some others might reply, "But James said we are justified by works and not by faith only" (James 2:24). And to both I reply, "Yes." Brethren, Paul and James are not contradicting one another.

Both James and Paul use Abraham as the example of the sort of faith that saves.

According to the Apostle Paul, the faith that saves is a specific quality of faith: "that faith of our father Abraham" (Romans 4:12). James contrasts the faith of Abraham to the faith of devils (James 2:19). Clearly, the faith that saves is not the sort of faith that devils have, but the sort of faith the Abraham had.

Paul points to the moment that Abraham believed God and God counted it to him for righteousness (Genesis 15:6; Romans 4:3). James points to the time when Abraham willingly offered up his son (James 2:21), and said Abraham's works proved the genuineness of his faith (James 2:18). Clearly, James is saying the faith that saves is the faith that produces works meet for repentance. This is exactly what Paul taught also (Acts 26:20).

In Ephesians 2:8-9, we find the very popular passage that declares we are saved by grace, through faith, and that not of ourselves, it is the gift of God, not of works lest any man should boast. Many fail to notice, however, that the next verse explains that this faith that saves is one that produces works: "For we are his workmanship, created in Christ Jesus unto good works" (Ephesians 2:10).

Jesus helps us understand the relationship of repentance to faith in John 3:16-21. The famous verse 16 declares, "For God so loved the world, that he gave his only begotten Son, that whosoever believeth in him should not perish but have everlasting life." Once again, few bother to pay attention to what follows. Read it below:

> For God sent not his Son into the world to condemn the world; but that the world through him might be saved. He that believeth on him is not condemned: but he that believeth not is condemned already, because he hath not believed in the name of the only begotten Son of God. And this is the condemnation, that light

is come into the world, and men loved darkness rather than light, because their deeds were evil. For every one that doeth evil hateth the light, neither cometh to the light, lest his deeds should be reproved. But he that doeth truth cometh to the light, that his deeds may be made manifest, that they are wrought in God. (John 3:17-21)

The word *repent* means to turn around. We have already seen that repentance is about turning around from darkness to light (Acts 26:20). Jesus explained that sinners are condemned because light has come into the world but they "loved darkness rather than light." In fact, He said they hate the light because their deeds are evil. So long as a sinner continues to love darkness and hate the light he will neither turn from darkness to the light nor from the power of Satan to God. Jesus goes on to say that those who do truth will come to the light. This is interesting because it does not say those who do righteousness, or those who do good works, will come to the light. It says those who do truth come to the light. Those who do truth will be honest about themselves, they will confess they are sinners, and they will turn to Christ Jesus for salvation and forgiveness. In order to turn to Christ, one must necessarily turn from Satan. This is repentance. Remember, godly sorrow works repentance in our heart.

Now, let's put this all together.

Jesus Christ has lighted every man that comes into the world (John 1:9). This is the lighting of the *candle of the Lord* (Proverbs 20:27) that searches the inward parts of the belly (Proverbs 20:27). The *belly* refers to our life in this flesh (I Corinthians 6:13). This candle of the Lord is our conscience (John 8:9; Romans 2:15). Additionally, God has dealt to every man the "measure of faith" (Romans 12:4).

Through His creation, God reveals Himself to every man, which stirs the faith that God has dealt to every man and serves to manifest God in them (Romans 1:17-21). Their conscience bears witness of their sin, and creation bears witness of their judge.

Jesus sent the Holy Spirit into the world to reprove it of sin, of righteousness, and of judgment (John 16:7-13). The point of reproving anyone is to appeal to his or her conscience.

God sent His Son to save sinners (John 3:16). Jesus said He would draw all men to Himself (John 12:32). When the gospel is preached, the Spirit of God stirs the measure of faith given to every sinner and reproves the conscience of sin (I Corinthians 14:24). Jesus then draws upon the heart of the sinner to come to Him for forgiveness.

The Father ponders the hearts of men as they respond to the gospel (Proverbs 21:2). Those who refuse to accept the witness of creation, or to receive the witness of their conscience concerning their sin, and so fail to believe on Jesus Christ are blinded from the glorious light of the gospel (II Corinthians 4:4). However, if the Father sees an honest and good heart of faith (Luke 8:15), and the sinner demonstrates godly sorrow, moving him to obey the command of God to repent (Acts 17:30), the Father will open the eyes of the sinner, and he or she will receive salvation.

There are many wonderful illustrations of this in Scripture. My favorite is the thief on the cross.

Two thieves were crucified with Jesus (Matthew 27:38). Both joined the crowd in cajoling Him (Matthew 27:44), until one of the thieves was repulsed by what he heard the other say. Something changed in his heart when he reflected on the fact that Jesus had done nothing to deserve the punishment He was suffering, but that he and the other thief deserved their condemnation (Luke 23:41). It is beautiful to notice that as soon as this man acknowledged his own sin, his eyes were opened, and he was enabled to see Jesus as the Messiah. He cried out to Jesus, "Lord, remember me when thou comest into thy kingdom" (Luke 23:42).

The Bible says if we confess with our mouth the Lord Jesus and believe in our heart that God raised Him from the dead, we will be saved (Romans 10:9). That is exactly what the repentant thief did. He confessed with his mouth that Jesus is Lord when he called Him "Lord." He declared faith in His resurrection when he said, "remember me when thou comest into thy kingdom." Romans 10:13

says, "For whosoever shall call upon the name of the Lord shall be saved." When the repentant thief called on the Lord to "remember me" he was calling on the Lord for salvation. Jesus said, "Verily I say unto thee, To day shalt thou be with me in paradise" (Luke 23:43).

Both thieves who were crucified with Jesus had been lighted when they came into the world (John 1:9). Both received the measure of faith dealt to every man (Romans 12:3). Jesus was dying for both of these men (I John 2:1-2). The Father desired both men to come to the knowledge of the truth (I Timothy 2:4). One loved darkness rather than light (John 3:17-21). And one of them reflected on their own sinfulness, and being moved by godly sorrow, repented (II Corinthians 7:11-14). When he repented in his heart, the Father opened his eyes to see Jesus as the Messiah, and he trusted Him as his personal Saviour.

Sadly, however, most of the new cart preachers purposely avoid bringing up the issue of repentance because they have decided to serve their own belly rather than serve the Lord (Philippians 3:19). Intuitively they know that most people recoil at the command of God to repent.

Some new cart pastors are afraid of their new cart Christian church members who have succumbed to the deceitfulness of riches and think gain is godliness and suppose that the best way to increase the offerings of the church and gain large crowds is to avoid preaching a negative message. These heap to themselves teachers that will tickle, or scratch, their itching ears (II Timothy 4:3).

Other new cart preachers are simpleminded, ignorant men who have not sought the Lord (Jeremiah 10:21) but have followed seducing spirits into grievous errors concerning the issue of repentance (I Timothy 4:1-4). They have not studied to show themselves approved unto God (II Timothy 2:15).

However, some good men avoid the topic of repentance because of how it has been distorted by those who teach the false doctrine called Lordship salvation.

Every Bible believer knows that no one is saved who does not confess Jesus is Lord (Romans 10:9). To confess with the mouth the Lord Jesus must be more than mere lip service because we know that "Many will say [to the Lord] in that day, Lord, Lord…And then will [He] profess unto them, I never knew you: depart from me ye that work iniquity" (Matthew 7:22-23). No one is saved who does not confess that Jesus Christ is in fact Lord of all.

An objection arises, however, when a teacher suggests that unless the sinner "makes Jesus Lord of his life" he cannot be saved. First, no where does the Bible say a sinner must "make Jesus Lord." Nor is it possible for anyone to do so. Jesus is Lord, and the sinner must confess it. Full surrender to the control of His Spirit and obedience to His Lordship is not a prerequisite to salvation; it is something that develops as we grow in grace and in the knowledge of our Lord Jesus Christ (II Peter 3:18).

Many who teach Lordship salvation use the story of the young man who asked Jesus, "What good thing shall I do that I may have eternal life" and claim that the Lord's answer is the plan of salvation (Matthew 19:16-26). If that is the case, then the price for salvation would be to keep selected portions of the Law, sell and distribute all that one has to the poor, and then to follow Jesus. Well, Zacchaeus got a better deal. He only had to sell half of his goods and give to the poor for salvation to come to his house (Luke 19:8). What nonsense. No one purchases salvation. Eternal life is the "gift of God" (Ephesians 2:8-9). As for Jesus' answer to that self-righteous young man, He was making the point that when it comes to meriting eternal life, "with men this is impossible; but with God, all things are possible" (Matthew 19:26).

Among those who avoid preaching repentance there are good men, with good hearts, like David; and as soon as they hear the truth they will receive it, repent, and start doing it right.

Chapter Eighteen

Salvation Without Regeneration

Question Twelve: *Do they preach salvation without regeneration?*

NEW CART PREACHING IS swelling the ranks of the many who will say "Lord, Lord" only to hear Jesus say, "I never knew you: depart from me" (Matthew 7:23). Preaching Christianity without Christ and forgiveness without repentance encourages people to believe they are saved who show no evidence of regeneration.

Regeneration is an act of God whereby He generates new life from death. We who were dead in trespasses and sins are quickened, that is, made alive by regeneration (Ephesians 2:1-5). Therefore, by regeneration we are saved from the penalty of sin, which is death, and from the judgment that follows (Romans 6:23; Hebrews 9:27). This is because God creates (generates into being) a new man in Christ Jesus (Ephesians 2:15) which is created in righteousness and true holiness (Ephesians 4:24). "Therefore, if any man be in Christ, he is a new creature: old things are passed away; behold, all things are become new" (II Corinthians 5:17). This means that if you are truly saved, that is, if you are a born-again Christian, you are a new person. We should expect anyone who has been regenerated to show some evidence of this new life.

Titus 3:5-7 says it is, "Not by works of righteousness which we have done, but according to His mercy he saved us, by the washing of regeneration, and renewing of the Holy Ghost..." We receive this glorious regeneration by grace through faith (Ephesians 2:8-9). It is not something we can earn, or achieve by personal reformation. It is a supernatural act of God that He mercifully bestows upon all who believe on His Son, the Lord Jesus Christ.

Salvation refers to our deliverance from the wrath to come (Matthew 3:7; I Thessalonians 1:10). Jesus said the wrath of God abides upon the unbeliever (John 3:36). He is angry with the wicked every day (Psalm 7:11). The wages of sin is death (Romans 6:23). After death there is a judgment (Hebrews 9:27). Jesus described the judgment vividly when He related the true story of a man who died and faced that judgment:

> The rich man also died and was buried; and in hell he lift up his eyes, being in torments, and seeth Abraham afar off, and Lazarus in his bosom. And he cried and said, Father Abraham, have mercy on me, and send Lazarus, that he may dip the tip of his finger in water, and cool my tongue; for I am tormented in this flame. (Luke 16:22b-24)

Death and hell will deliver up the dead that are in them and all who are lost (not saved) will stand before the Almighty at the Great White Throne for their final judgment (Revelation 20:11-15). From here they will be cast into the Lake of Fire where they will suffer everlasting punishment (Matthew 25:46).

The Lake of Fire was created by God as the only place in His universe fitting for sinners where their sin can never again inflict injury upon any innocent person, or upon His creation. Remember, it all got started down here with one seemingly minor infraction of God's Law: Adam and Eve ate of the forbidden fruit (Genesis 3). But look where it led: Cain murdered his brother, Abel (Genesis 4). God will not allow sin to ruin His new Heaven and new earth (Revelation 21:1-2; 8).

What is the *washing of regeneration* that saves us? This expression refers to the washing away of our sins by the blood of Christ Jesus (Revelation 1:5-6).

Preaching Christianity without Christ and forgiveness without repentance results in people believing they are saved who have not received the washing of regeneration and the renewing of the Holy Ghost: hence, salvation without regeneration. It behooves all of us to "give diligence to make [our] calling and election sure" (II Peter 1:10). Many will say to Him on the day of their judgment, "Lord, Lord, have we not prophesied in thy name? and in thy name have cast out devils? and in thy name done many wonderful works? And [Jesus] will profess unto them, I never knew you: depart from me, ye that work iniquity" (Matthew 7:22-23).

New cart preachers allow sinners who refuse to depart from iniquity to imagine that they are saved, that they are Christians. Sadly, they are swelling the ranks of that crowd to whom Jesus will say, "I never knew you: depart from me, ye that work iniquity" (Matthew 7:22-23). Jesus did say there would be *many*. Selah![34]

---

34 The term *Selah* is usually interpreted to mean *pause and consider.* It is used often in the Psalms (Psalm 3:2, 4. 6, and 69 more). Its meaning is not delineated in Scripture, but is deduced from the fact that it names a city in the Valley of Salt where significant ancient wars were fought (I Kings 14:7; II Samuel 8:13; I Chronicles 18:12; 25:11). From these verses we note it is identified with Edom and Syria, or Idumea, in a valley below the Dead Sea. Along with the Valley of Jehoshaphat (Joel 3:2, 12), which is Armageddon (Revelation 16:16), the Valley of Salt will play a very significant role in the Day of the Lord. In Isaiah 34:1-10, it is described as being the scene of a mighty battle in the end, where God makes it brimstone and burning pitch (Isaiah 34:9). From this it is believed the term *Selah* is intended to evoke serious contemplation of the judgment of the Almighty God. Hence, *pause and consider!*

Chapter Nineteen

Politics
Without God

Question Thirteen: *Do they alienate God from politics in the minds and hearts of their congregation?*

UNREASONABLE AND WICKED MEN labor incessantly to pull America out from under God (II Thessalonians 3:2). New cart preachers are among their most effective and constant allies, fulfilling William Booth's famous prediction that God would be removed from politics in the twentieth century.[35]

Most new cart Christians subscribe to the lie that preachers are not supposed to preach on political subjects, even when they involve moral issues. Some go so far as to say Christians are not supposed to be involved in politics. Virtually every new cart Christian believes their faith is supposed to be separated from their politics. And new cart pastors have been willing accomplices in perpetuating this lie.

Our Founders repeatedly warned us that without the Christian religion, our freedoms would soon be lost.

Christians during the war for independence did not believe the way so many do today. The pulpits were aflame with passionate preaching about freedom, liberty, and the truth that Jesus Christ is LORD over all the nations of the earth. And who is surprised? No one

---

35 *Op. Cit.* Booth

can read the Bible without noticing repeated declarations from God regarding virtually every nation under the sun. We certainly have a message to the nations.

Every evil that is troubling our culture today is being advanced by unreasonable and wicked men and women through our political institutions (II Thessalonians 3:2). Yet all Satan has to do these days is to call something political and most Christians get quiet and think they have nothing to say about it. This lie has put Christians to sleep. I say, "Now it is high time to awake out of sleep" (Romans 13:11).

One way to help new cart Christians rub the sleep out of their eyes is to dispel the following myths that Satan has used to keep Christians out of his way while he took control of our government:

First myth: *Romans 13:1-6 teaches that all government officials are ordained by God and given carte blanche power over our lives.* Romans 13:1-6 teaches us to respect and honor the higher powers with our submission to their divine right to rule us because all power is ordained by God. However, this does not mean everyone holding that power is ordained of God. For example, Hosea 8:4 says, "They have set up kings, but not by me." God complained against Israel because they put persons in *the power* God ordained who were not ordained by Him to hold it.

No human authority is absolute. When the authorities commanded the apostles to not preach any more in Jesus' Name, they replied, "We ought to obey God rather than men" (Acts 5:29). What will these Christians do who believe this myth when the government says you can no longer pray in Jesus' Name in public? It's already happening in some quarters of the so-called *public square.*[36] By their own rule of interpreting Romans 13, they will be compelled to comply. This interpretation of Romans 13 has confused many sincere believers, but for some it is a convenient fig leaf used to cover their spiritual cowardice. We must face the fact that many give lip service to Jesus Christ who in practice bow to the god of this world.

---

36 Limbaugh, David, <u>Persecution: How Liberals are Waging War Against Christianity</u>, pages 149-265.

It's important to rightly understand Romans 13:1-6. The same word that is translated *power* in Romans 13 is also translated *power* in Matthew 28:18, where Jesus said, "All power is given unto me in Heaven and in earth." Since all power in Heaven and in earth has been given to Jesus Christ, He is the divine ordaining authority behind of all human authority. No human authority is above Jesus Christ the King.

Jesus ordained the power to serve a specific purpose. The role of the power is to execute wrath upon evildoers (Romans 13:4). Obviously, the meaning of the word *evildoers* is to be understood within the context of this passage. When governments turn their sword against the righteous, they have defied their ordaining power (authority) and Christians ought to rebuke them. Our "sword" is the Word of God, and we should use it to reprove and rebuke any government that disobeys the ordaining authority of their power.

Second myth: *The Bible teaches separation of church and state.* The church has been given the keys of the kingdom of Christ Jesus (Matthew 16:17) and the Sword of the Spirit (Ephesians 6:18). As ambassadors for Christ (II Corinthians 5:20), and as good soldiers (II Timothy 2:3), we war a spiritual warfare against the principalities, and powers, and the rulers of the darkness of this world (Ephesians 6:10-19). We preach the gospel of the kingdom of God (Matthew 24:14), commanding all men everywhere to repent and believe on Jesus Christ as Lord (Acts 17:30; Romans 10:9-13). By preaching the gospel of the kingdom, the church uses the keys to open the door of Christ's kingdom to every nation that obeys the gospel of Jesus Christ.

If a nation surrenders to the command of Christ, and to His righteousness, that nation will be blessed and exalted (Psalm 33:12; Proverbs 14:34). Christ, walking in the midst of His churches (Revelation 1:20; 2:1) will give to that nation His kingdom authority and blessing. One great example of this is the mystery of America's rise to world glory and power. (Of course, her decline is also testimony of the truth that such nations that forget God are turned into hell (Psalm 9:17).)

However, the church has not been given the carnal, that is, the physical sword of civil government. We fight a spiritual war with spiritual weapons (II Corinthians 10:4).

The separation doctrine was supposed to serve as a protection of the freedom of the conscience and liberty of the soul. A man must be free from human coercion to believe according to the dictates of his own conscience. The separation doctrine was supposed to ensure that the government would not give to any particular church the sword of civil government to be used to force conformity to any particular doctrine or religion.

Nevertheless, every government is subject to Christ Jesus and every Christian is duty bound, as His ambassador, to represent His kingdom to the kingdoms of this world. Separation notwithstanding, we have an obligation to preach the gospel of the kingdom (declaring Jesus Christ is LORD and King over all the kingdoms of the earth). We have an obligation to preach to all nations the commandments of the King of kings, and LORD of lords (Matthew 28:18-20). Therefore, we must speak to the sins of nations and rebuke all rulers of the darkness of this world (Ephesians 5:11), warning them of the soon return of the King. Selah!

Under the influence of Satan, the children of disobedience have twisted the doctrine of separation into the false doctrine that Christians have no part in world affairs. They view Christians and Christianity as an otherworldly philosophy that might have meaning to persons individually, but has no authority or right to exert any influence in their world. Many Christians accept this idea. They are content to sit on the sidelines, believing that the world belongs to Satan and the children of disobedience (Ephesians 2:2). This is a lie.

The best way to understand our role on the earth and our relationship to the children of disobedience is to consider Jesus' parable given in Luke 19:11-27 (also see Matthew 25:14-36).

Because so many of His followers thought that His kingdom would immediately appear, He explained how the coming of His kingdom would occur.

He likens His kingdom to a "certain nobleman" leaving his domain to the stewardship of his servants, while he goes away to receive for himself a kingdom. While he was gone, these stewards were to "occupy" until He returned (Luke 19:13). However, while the "certain nobleman" was gone, his citizens revolted against his authority, and sent word to him declaring, "We will not have this man to reign over us" (Luke 19:14).

Next, He explains what happened when the "certain nobleman" returned having obtained the kingdom. First, he judged his servants for their faithfulness or lack thereof (Luke 19:15-26). Then he turned his attention to those citizens who declared they would not have him to reign over them and commanded: "But those mine enemies which would not that I should reign over them, bring hither, and slay them before me" (Luke 19:27). Let's interpret this parable.

Obviously, Jesus is the "certain nobleman." The servants represent the followers of Jesus Christ in whom is the Spirit of Christ Who cries Abba, Father (Galatians 4:6). But who are the citizens that rebel against His right to rule them (Luke 19:14)?

Remember that Jesus purchased the entire earth when He died on the Cross for the sins of the world (Matthew 13:38, 44; I John 2:1-2; Colossians 2:14-15). At the beginning of Christ's earthly ministry, He encountered Satan in the desert who declared that all the kingdoms of the world and the glory of them had been given to him (Luke 4). Jesus did not dispute Satan's claim. It was true! Satan offered all the kingdoms of the world to Jesus if only He would bow and worship Satan (Luke 4; Matthew 4). Our Lord refused. However, after Jesus rose from the dead, He declared, "All power is given unto me in Heaven and in earth" (Matthew 28:18). Colossians 2:14-15 reveals that upon the Cross Jesus spoiled all principalities and powers (Romans 13:1-6; Ephesians 3:10; 6:12; Titus 3:1; Colossians 1:16). He displaced Satan from his place in the earth (John 12:31-32).

Now, Satan operates as the prince of the power of the air and extends his influence in the world as the spirit that works in the children of disobedience (Ephesians 2:2). These children of disobedience are the "citizens" of the earth who refuse to submit to the right of Christ to rule them.

Jesus delivered His goods to His servants (Matthew 25:14). This would include the gospel of the kingdom and the power of His Spirit to preach this gospel with Christ's authority.

The gospel of the kingdom declares what I bring out above, namely, that Jesus Christ died for the sins of all mankind, was buried and arose from the grave the third day (I Corinthians 15:1-3), thereby spoiling all principality and power; and He is now the King over all of Heaven and earth. He has left the earth (Acts 1:9-11) to receive for Himself a kingdom (Revelation 11:15) and will return to rule the earth with a rod of iron (Revelation 19:11-21; 20:1-6).

Meanwhile, He left the keys of the kingdom with His church. In His absence, His servants are to be His salt to the earth and light to the world (Matthew 5:13-14). Being salt and light includes commanding all men everywhere to repent and believe on Jesus Christ (Acts 17:30; Romans 10:9-13).[37] As ambassadors for Christ, we are His representatives to the kingdoms of this world (II Corinthians 5:20).

All of God's prophets have spoken to the sins of the nations of this world. Isaiah, Jeremiah, Ezekiel, Daniel, all of them. John the Baptist spoke against the personal sins of King Herod, accusing him for the sin of adultery when he took his brother's wife (Mark 6:18). Paul challenged civil authorities when they violated the law (Acts 22:25). They denounced the evils of politicians in their day, and cried, "Thus saith the Lord" as they laid out God's judgment against them. The spirit of antichrist has done a good job seducing many Christians into becoming the evil servants Jesus spoke against in the parable we looked at earlier.

The church must speak to the politics and to the politicians of their generation wherever these defy the authority of Christ the King.

---

37 Consider the significance that the command of the gospel is to "confess with thy mouth the *Lord* Jesus" (Romans 10:9–emphasis added). It means the sinner must renounce his allegiance to Satan and declare his surrender to the right of Jesus to rule the earth as Lord (Acts 26:18).

Chapter Twenty

Trimming

Question Fourteen: *Do they trim their message to appeal to the world?*

YOU KNOW YOU ARE in a new cart church if it encourages the practice of trimming. Jeremiah asked the believers in his day who strayed off the ancient paths into new ones (Jeremiah 18:15), "Why trimmest thou thy way to seek love?" (Jeremiah 2:33a). The Jews were trimming their ways to fit in with the world around them, to gain favor with their pagan neighbors. It's true that God so loved the world that He gave His only begotten Son (John 3:16), however, He very specifically commanded us to "love not the world" (I John 2:15). New cart Christians trim their lifestyles and their messages to gain the favor of the world.

Christians trim their ways when they adopt worldly manners and customs in order to fit in with the world. We certainly may wear fashionable attire for our own comfort and to our own tastes. But Christians often fail to consider that some of the fashions, customs, and manners of the people in the world are antichrist by design.

The spirit that operates in the children of disobedience hates the Spirit of Jesus Christ their Creator. Therefore, that spirit leads those under its influence to disfigure the image of God given to them, for example, with piercings. Some of their fashions are specifically adapted to publicly exhibit their moral corruptions as brute beasts (Jude 10), sporting animal-like hairstyles, for example. More obvious is the passion evident among many to publicly display their own nakedness, which is to their shame (Exodus 32:25). It's as if the spirit in them seeks reverse sanctification, that is, Satan wants those under the control of his spirit to be peculiarly unchristian. It's as if they purposely set themselves apart from any identification with holiness, or purity, or godliness.

Absurdly, many Christians follow fashions that are designed by the children of disobedience to dishonor Christ. Rather than dress to identify with Christ, they dress in fashions designed to shame Him. For example, you will notice Christians adopting fashions made popular by some of the most vile and wicked people in the entertainment industry.

The same is true with their speech and manners. Some Christians proudly borrow expressions that were contrived by the world for the specific purpose of offending God.

The point here is not that Christians are obliged to dress up to go to church. Although something should be said about the fact that there are new cart Christians who are as focused on outward appearance as those they accuse of this sin. I've visited new cart churches where I was openly derided for wearing a suit. Not teasingly, but with scorn. Of course, I could argue that how we dress expresses our attitude, and that those who mock me for wearing a suit to church would probably not dress to meet the President the way they dress to meet with fellow believers for worship. Interestingly, I did not notice what that brother was wearing to church. What a joke the devil has played on Christians. Ironically, here you had a fellow mocking another for dressing up for church whose basis for doing so is that God does not look on the outward appearance (II Corinthians 10:7).

The important point is that adapting yourself to worldly attire to reach sinners is definitely contrary to the spirit and teaching of the Bible (II Corinthians 6:17). Indeed, the spirit that operates in them moves them to develop fashions that offend the sensibilities of our

Holy God. And the Spirit that is in us is grieved when we fail to be holy, that is, publicly separated from the world and unashamedly identified with God.

You trim the gospel when you leave out any part of the message you are afraid might be offensive to the sinner. For example, many down play or totally ignore the issue of sin when witnessing to sinners. But remember, when Jesus spoke to the woman at the well (John 4), He directly confronted her conscience with a reproof for her sins. She was being cavalier in her attitude toward Him. But when He brought up her personal sin, she became very serious. This is what the Bible says will happen when we preach the true Word of God: "But if all prophesy (preach)" to a sinner he is "convinced of all, he is judged of all: and thus are the secrets of his heart made manifest" (I Corinthians 14:24-25).

However, the new cart Christian avoids confronting sinners with their sins. The new cart Christian diminishes the issue of sin as if it is a mere technicality. Or they will neutralize conviction as much as possible, saying things such as, "Well, of course, we are all sinners." Of course, confessing the truth that we are all sinners is appropriate but the tone must be one that communicates the seriousness of this problem, and not one that suggests it's no big deal because every body does it.

The reason many new cart Christians don't zero in on the issue of sin is that they are cavalier about sin in their own lives. But most new cart Christians avoid the issue of personal sin because it is likely to make the sinner uncomfortable.

Some avoid the issue of sin because they don't want to appear judgmental. Yet Jesus, who said "judge not, that ye be not judged" (Matthew 7:1), said also, "but judge righteous judgment" (John 7:24). Declaring God's truth to sinners is not being "judgmental"; it's being truthful. These new cart Christians unwittingly end up doing nothing more than adding yet another member to that crowd who will cry "Lord, Lord" only to hear Jesus say, "I never knew you" (Matthew 7:22-23).

New cart pastors, with the help of the new cart Christians who follow them, have created churches that are large dog kennels and pig farms (II Peter 2:22), rather than pastures for Christ's sheep (John 21:16). The true sheep are scattered and starved, and many of them are snared in these new cart churches (Jeremiah 10:21). Jesus laments that they are "as sheep without a shepherd" (Matthew 9:36).

Chapter Twenty-One

The Chief Shepherd's Call

BEFORE JUDAH LOST HER kingdom, the Spirit of Christ (I Peter 1:11) through Jeremiah called out to them: "Thus saith the LORD, Stand ye in the ways, and see, and ask for the old paths, where is the good way, and walk therein, and ye shall find rest for your souls" (Jeremiah 6:16a). According to the Apostle Paul, Christ, through Jeremiah, was calling on His sheep today to return to the old paths (I Corinthians 10:11).

Jesus said, "My sheep hear my voice and follow me" (John 10:27). He uses the word *sheep* to represent His own, to whom He has given eternal life (John 10:28). By calling us sheep, He identifies us with Him in a very personal way, as He is the sacrificial Lamb of God Who died for us and yet lives (John 1:29; Revelation 5:6). We've already pointed out that there are many who claim to be His who are not (Matthew 7:22-23). John spoke of those who in every way appeared to be one of the household of faith but later were exposed as false believers (I John 2:19; II Corinthians 11:26; Galatians 2:4). Jesus said one thing that distinguishes His sheep from any others is that they hear His voice, and follow Him.

Christ Jesus gave us His Spirit to dwell in us and to guide us to all truth (John 16:13). Many genuine Christians wander out in the wilderness without pasture, tangled up in a new cart church.

So, why do they stay in a new cart church?

Some stay because they are snared, tangled up with the new cart church and feel trapped. Perhaps the snare that holds them is fear (I Timothy 1:8). It's what they know and they are afraid to try something different. Perhaps their connection to friends or family has snared them in a new cart church (Matthew 10:37; Proverbs 29:25). Maybe some stay out of a sense of loyalty, or duty (Acts 5:29; Colossians 3:24). Many genuine, born-again Christians are tangled up in new cart churches as teachers, or they are serving on this or that committee or program, and they feel they have an obligation to stay. Or perhaps they are afraid they will not find such opportunities elsewhere. Others stay because of denominational loyalty.

Yet all believers know that Jesus is their only LORD (John 13:13), and that if there is a conflict between serving men or God, they should obey God rather than men (Acts 5:29).

Typically, snared sheep are unhappy, uneasy with what they see going on, grieved about the lack of conviction and the lack of genuine deep Scripture teaching, and they are becoming increasingly discontented with the shallowness of the ministry they support.

Jesus calls on all His sheep who are snared in these new cart churches to break free of the snares that hold them there and find an old path church to support with their time, talent, and treasure. God calls on you right now to stand in the way, and to see and ask for the old paths where is the good way. And He promises that then you will find rest for your soul.

However, there are some genuine Christians who attend new cart churches because they walk after the flesh and not after the spirit (Romans 8:5). In other words, a new cart church is comfortable to them specifically because it is carnal, fleshly, and worldly. They are snared in their own flesh.

Often new cart Christians are vain, and proud, and they stay because they like being identified with what appears to be a thriving, successful ministry. Perhaps they derive some personal esteem by being connected with a large church.

This is not to say all large churches are necessarily new cart. Some of the greatest and largest churches in America today are old path churches. Lancaster Baptist Church, in Lancaster, CA, averages above 5,000 and is pastored by an old path preacher, Dr. Paul Chappell. In Hammond, Indiana, an old path preacher, Dr. John Wilkerson, pastors First Baptist Church with an average attendance above 10,000. While there are many notable exceptions, typically, most old path churches are smaller, struggling congregations.

Many of Christ's sheep are spiritually sick, and being carnal they will say of an old path church, "We love the preaching and the teaching, and we really appreciate the product we see in the young people and the quality of the members," and then comes the *but*. "But you don't have the cool activities for the teens," or "But you don't have a very nice church campus," or "But it looks like you are struggling to get along." It's particularly disturbing when they preface their *buts* with, "The (*new cart*) church down the street does not teach what we believe and the preaching is shallow, but …" See what I mean? The things that ultimately decide for them what church they will attend are not the things that matter most to God. They are the things that matter most to the flesh. These Christians savor the things that are of men rather the things that are of God.

In many instances, it's the fleshly appetites of their children or other family members that Satan uses to snare them in a new cart church. They would go to an old path church, but their children rebel and so they find a compromising church that will accommodate the spirit of rebellion controlling their children.

New cart Christian homes often are not led by the husband as the Bible teaches they should be (Ephesians 5:22; Colossians 3:18; I Corinthians 11:1-3). Many homes are oppressed (tyrannized, driven) by the children's wishes, and under the rule of the woman (Isaiah 3:12). Such children and such women do not like old path churches.

Christians who walk after the flesh and not after the Spirit are comfortable in new cart churches. They don't feel comfortable in old path churches where their rebellion against the Lord is challenged.

To become a Christian you must "confess with your mouth" that Jesus is Lord (Romans 10:9). It is apparent that for many it was mere lip service, for they are among those who call Him Lord but do not the things that He says (Luke 6:46). Many will say "Lord, Lord," to whom Jesus will say, "I never knew you" (Matthew 7:23). Perhaps you know Christians who "draweth nigh unto [Him] with their mouth...but their heart is far from [Him]" (Matthew 15:8).

The Chief Shepherd is calling His sheep to "come out of her my people" (Revelation 18:4). Soon the tares will be gathered and separated from among the wheat. The tares will be bundled to be burned; that is, set apart for judgment. The wheat, however, will be gathered into His barn, the true church (Matthew 13:25-30; Hebrews 12:23).

My dear friend, I hope you are already serving Christ Jesus in an old path church. If, however, you have discovered that you are in a new cart church, and you are sensible that the voice of the Chief Shepherd is calling you to get into an old path church, please read the next chapter carefully. It explains the first step you must take to return to the old paths, where is the good way.

You must make your calling and election sure (II Peter 1:10).

Chapter Twenty-Two

The Old Path Gospel

The first step to return to the old paths is to make your own calling and election sure (II Peter 1:10).

JESUS TOLD HIS DISCIPLES to go into the entire world and preach the gospel to every creature (Mark 16:15). **The gospel is God's message that Jesus died for our sins, according to the Scriptures (the Bible), was buried, and rose again the third day according to the Scriptures** (I Corinthians 15:1-3).

Why did Jesus die and rise from the dead?

According to the Scriptures, He did this in order to "seek and to save [the] lost" (Luke 19:10; John 10:15-17).

> For the Son of man is come to seek and to save that which was lost.
> Luke 19:10

How was mankind "lost" to God?

God's most powerful Angel, Lucifer, was perfect in wisdom and beauty until iniquity (unrighteousness) was found in him ([1] Ezekiel 28:13-19). Although God gave him great riches, glory, and power, he began to envy God's greater riches, glory, and power. The first lie was birthed in Lucifer's

> 1. Ezekiel 28:15 "Thou wast perfect in thy ways from the day that thou wast created, till iniquity was found in thee.

heart when he deceived himself into believing that he would lift his throne above the stars of God and become, "like the Most High" ([2]Isaiah 14:12-17; John 8:44). He deceived one-third of the heavenly host of angels into joining him in his rebellion ([3]Revelation 12:4). God took the dust of the earth and formed a creature inferior to the angels, called man; and from the man, He made the woman, and gave to them what Lucifer coveted (lusted for)—the image and likeness of God ([4]Genesis 1:26,27). Their names were Adam and Eve, and they lived in a garden called Eden. And Lucifer hated them (Genesis 1-3).

2. Isaiah 14:14 "I will ascend above the heights of the clouds; I will be like the most High.

3. Revelation 12:4 "And his tail drew the third part of the stars of Heaven, and did cast them to the earth

4. Genesis 1:27 "So God created man in his own image, in the image of God created he him; male and female created he them.

God loved Adam and Eve. He expected them to do what gratefulness and conscience would require—to love Him in return ([5]Matthew 22:37; I John 4:8). God cannot lie ([6]Titus 1:2), and He would not pretend they loved Him unless they were free to choose. God showed His love by granting to them the gift of free will. In this way, they could, in their turn, show their love for Him by yielding their will to Him in obedience ([7]John 14:15; Genesis 2:17). He warned them that the consequence of disobedience would be death ([8]Romans 6:23; Genesis 2:17).

5. Matthew 22:37 "Jesus said unto him, Thou shalt love the Lord thy God with all thy heart, and with all thy soul, and with all thy mind.

6. Titus 1:2 "... God, that cannot lie,

7. John 14:15 "If ye love me, keep my commandments.

8. Romans 6:23 "For the wages of sin is death.

God would test man. Making man in God's image did not mean God gave to man all of God's attributes (characteristics). For example, God did not make man omnipotent (all powerful) or omniscient (all knowing). One of the characteristics of God that He did not immediately give to man, but that He intended for man to have in His time, was the knowledge of good and evil. God placed the tree of the knowledge of good and evil in the garden, within the reach of Adam and Eve, and commanded them not to eat of its fruit. Remembering the backdrop to this is Lucifer's own evil coveting of God's image and likeness, we can appreciate the appropriateness of this test of man's love. Adam and Eve would soon show whether or not they would follow Lucifer's example, who coveted God's likeness, and sin against God's Law to get it.

Lucifer entered into the garden and lied to Eve ([9]John 8:44). He told her that God prohibited her from eating of that fruit because He did not want her to be as God, "knowing good and evil" (Genesis 3:5). Further, he told her that she would not surely die if she ate of the fruit. Eve believed his lie, and disobeyed her Creator ([10]I Timothy 2:14). Then she offered the fruit to her husband, and he joined her in disobedience (sin) against God.

9. John 8:44 "... the devil, ... is a liar, and the father of it.
10. 1Timothy 2:14 "And Adam was not deceived, but the woman being deceived was in the transgression.

Because Adam and Eve ate the fruit in disobedience to God, the evil aspect of that fruit dominated in their knowledge of good and evil. Man's nature was corrupted, and they opened the door to death ([11]Romans 5:12,13).

11. Romans 5:12 Wherefore, as by one man sin entered into the world, and death by sin; and so death passed upon all men, for that all have sinned

Death occurs physically when our soul (life) is separated from our body ([12]Genesis 35:18). It occurs spiritually when our spirit is separated from our God ([13]Ephesians 2:1; Isaiah 59:2). Immediately, they died spiritually. Physically, they began the process of aging that ends in death.

12. Genesis 35:18 "And it came to pass, as her soul was in departing, (for she died)
13. Ephesians 2:1 "And you hath he quickened, who were dead in trespasses and sins

Even more devastating was the fact that the nature of man was corrupted by his sin. This corrupted nature, and its consequence, death, was passed on to all Adam's descendants through his seed ([See] [11]Romans 5:12). Therefore, sin and death are resident in the body of all born of Adam ([14]Romans 7:18), which spiritually makes them children of Lucifer (Satan, or the Devil) ([15]I John 3:10; Revelation 12:9). For this reason, all who die in their sins will face the same judgment prepared for Satan and his angels—to be cast alive into the Lake of Fire that burns with fire and brimstone for eternity ([16]Matthew 25:41; Revelation 14:10; 20:10-15).

Perhaps you think it is unfair for God to allow the penalty of death to pass on to all Adam's descendants. We see this principle at work in many ways. The addicted mother passes her addiction to the child in her womb. It's not the fault of the child, but the relationship between the mother and child is such that the behavior of the sinful mother has a direct impact upon the innocent child. However, we must remember that God did not create sin in man, and it was not His desire that man would sin. He exposed His creation to this vanity in hope ([17]Romans 8:20). But consider the wisdom and mercy of God. Because sin and death entered into the world through the sin of one man, God may justly deliver all from sin and death through the righteousness of one man ([18]Romans 5:13-19).

14. Romans 7:18 "In my flesh dwelleth no good thing."

15. I John 3:10 "In this the children of God are manifest, and the children of the devil: whosoever doeth not righteousness is not of God."

16. Matthew 25:41 "Then shall he say also unto them on the left hand, Depart from me, ye cursed, into everlasting fire, prepared for the devil and his angels."

17. Romans 8:20 "For the creature was made subject to vanity, not willingly, but by reason of him who hath subjected the same in hope.

18. Romans 5:18,(19) As by the offence of one judgment came upon all... so by the righteousness of one the free gift came upon all.

God will not allow even one sin to enter into Heaven; look at what it has done down here. Especially grievous is how sin hurts the innocent. Therefore, God has decreed that all who die in their sins must go to hell, where sin can never again hurt the innocent ([19]Hebrews 9:27; [20]II Thessalonians 1:8). That is the story of how mankind was *lost* to God. And that is why mankind needs a Saviour.

19. Hebrews 9:27 "And as it is appointed unto men once to die, but after this the judgment.
20. II Thessalonians 1:8 "In flaming fire taking vengeance on them that know not God, and that obey not the gospel of our Lord Jesus Christ.

How did God bring salvation to mankind?

There is nothing man can do to make up for his sins, or to remove them from before God. In God's eyes, even our righteousness is no better than filthy rags ([21]Isaiah 64:6; Titus 3:5). Who then can be saved? Jesus said that with men, this is impossible; but with God, all things are possible ([22]Matthew 19:24-26).

21. Isaiah 64:6 "But we are all as an unclean thing, and all our righteousnesses are as filthy rags; and we all do fade as a leaf; and our iniquities, like the wind, have taken us away."
22. Matthew 19:25-26
  His disciples [said], Who then can be saved?
  Jesus ... said unto them, With men this is impossible; but with God all things are possible."

The Bible says that if by one man's sin, all were made sinners, then by one man's righteousness all could be made righteous (Romans 5:19). If somehow we could be born again, from a sinless "Adam," we would then have a sinless nature. The good news of the gospel is that God made it possible for us to be born again of a sinless "Adam."

God sent Christ (means the Anointed One) into the world to save sinners. According to the Bible, Christ is the eternal image of the invisible God, the express image of His Person ([23]Hebrews 1:3; Colossians 1:15). Before He came to the earth, He was in the form of God ([24]Philippians 2:5).

23. Hebrews 1:3 "Who being the brightness of his glory, and the express image of his person.
24. Philippians 2:5-6
  Who, being in the form of God

In this way, Christ is to God what our body is to us ([25]I Thessalonians 5:23). Christ is the expression of God, and as such, He is called the "Word" ([26]John 1:1,14). Also, the Word is called God's Seed ([27]I Peter 1:23; Galatians 3:16). God joined His Seed (the Word) with the seed of a woman named Mary. The child thus conceived was both the Son of man and the Son of God (John 1:1,14; Philippians 2:5-11). By joining His Seed (the Word) with the woman's seed, God bypassed the corruption of sin that was in Adam's seed (John 1:1,14). This produced a new sinless man, the only begotten Son of God, Whom the Bible says is God manifest in the flesh ([28]I Timothy 3:16). The Bible refers to this new man as the "Last Adam" ([29]I Corinthians 15:45). God commanded that His Name would be Jesus, because He would save His people from their sins ([30]Matthew 1:21). Here is how.

Being the Son of man, He could represent mankind before God. And because He was a man He could die on man's behalf, thus paying the wages of sin ([31]Romans 6:23; 5:8). However, because He was the Son of God, He was sinless, which means the life in His blood ([32]Leviticus 17:11) was without sin. Therefore, when He died on the Cross, it was not for His sins. Because He was without sin, He did not have to go into hell fire after He died. Instead, He had the right to reclaim His body from death and rise from the

25. I Thessalonians 5:23 your whole spirit and soul and body

26. John 1:1,14 "In the beginning was the Word, and the Word was with God, and the Word was God. ... And the Word was made flesh, and dwelt among us.

27. 1Peter 1:23 "Being born again, not of corruptible seed, but of incorruptible, by the Word of God, which liveth and abideth for ever.

28. 1Timothy 3:16 "God was manifest in the flesh."

29. 1Corinthians 15:45 "The first man Adam was made a living soul; the last Adam was made a quickening spirit.

30. Matthew 1:21 "Thou shalt call his name JESUS: for he shall save his people from their sins.

31. Romans 6:23 "For the wages of sin is death... .

32. Leviticus 17:11 "For the life of the flesh is in the blood

grave ([33]John 10:17). And His blood was accepted as payment in full for the sins of man so that all who receive God's Son are washed (exonerated) from their own sins ([34]Revelation 1:5; Ephesians 1:7; Hebrews 9:12).

According to the Bible, the life (*soul*) of man is in the blood ([See 32]Leviticus 17:11). The *soul* is made up of two aspects, the *psuche* (translated *soul*, from which we get the word psyche), and *zoe* (which refers to the fundamental principle of *life*). When we believe on Jesus, we believe to the saving of our *soul* ([35]Hebrews 10:39). What happens is very simple, and yet profound. Our soul (*psyche*) is washed from sin, and our life (*zoe*) is removed and hid with Christ in God (Colossians 3:3).

If our *life* is removed, how is it that we live? Paul answered this question in [37]Galatians 2:20. He explained that although we are "crucified with Christ" (meaning we have died with Him), we live, "yet not I, but Christ liveth (*zoe*) in me."

God the Father has decreed that all who receive His Son will be given the power to become a child of God ([38]John 1:11-13). Here is how that happens.

33. John 10:17
Therefore doth my Father love me, because I lay down my life, that I might take it again.

34. Revelation 1:5 "And from Jesus Christ, who loved us, and washed us from our sins in his own blood.

35. Hebrews 10:39 believe to the saving of the soul.

37. Galatians 2:20 "I am crucified with Christ: nevertheless I live; yet not I, but Christ liveth in me: and the life which I now live in the flesh I live by the faith of the Son of God, who loved me, and gave himself for me.

38. John 1:11-13 "... But as many as received him, to them gave he power to become the sons of God.

39. Galatians 3:27 "For as many of you as have been baptized into Christ have put on Christ.

When we receive Jesus Christ, the Spirit of God removes us from Adam and places us into Christ ([39]Galatians 3:27; I Corinthians 12:13). As in Adam we inherited death, so now in Christ we receive the free gift of eternal life ([See 40 next page] John 10:28; I John 5:12-13). Because the life we receive from Jesus is sinless, and eternal, all who receive this life are eternally saved from hell fire ([41]Romans 5:9; Hebrews 10:39).

And this is the reason it is called the *gospel*; the word means *good news.* Indeed, it is good news that Jesus Christ has died for our sins, according to the Scriptures, and that He was buried and arose again, according to the Scriptures, and that all who believe the gospel will be saved from hell and given eternal life ([42]I Corinthians 15:1-3).

What does it mean to believe the gospel?

Believing on Jesus means you are trusting in Him, and in Him alone, to save you.[43] He said, "I am the way, the truth, and the life: no man cometh unto the Father, but by me" (John 14:6). You must not trust in any church to save you – Baptist, Protestant, or Catholic. Nor should you trust in any baptism, or in your own good works, or in any other religion. **You must trust in the Name of Jesus alone as your only hope for salvation.**[44]

40. John 10:28 "And I give unto them eternal life; and they shall never perish ...."

41. Romans 5:9 "we shall be saved from wrath through him

42. I Corinthians 15:1-3 "I declare unto you the gospel. ... For I delivered unto you first of all that which I also received, how that Christ died for our sins according to the scriptures; and that he was buried, and that he rose again the third day according to the scriptures.

43. Proverbs 3:5 "Trust in the LORD with all thine heart ... .
44. Acts 4:12 "There is none other name whereby we must be saved.
45. John 1:12 "But as many as received him, to them gave he power to become the sons of God

If you trust Him, then you will receive Him ([45]John 1:11-13). To receive Him means you acknowledge that Jesus Christ is Lord, which, of course, includes acknowledgment that you surrender yourself to Him as your Lord. Receiving Him means you accept Him as God's provision for your salvation, believing the gospel (explained above), and trusting that when you receive Jesus Christ, your sins are washed away by the blood He shed on Calvary

(⁴⁶Revelation 1:5). According to the Bible, the moment you by faith receive Jesus Christ, you are birthed to God by the Word of His Spirit (⁴⁷I Peter 1:23; John 1:11-13). Then you are no longer a child of the Devil, but instead, at the very moment that you put your trust in Him, you become a child of God (⁴⁸Galatians 4:6; John 1:12).

Why some miss the gospel, and how to make certain you have not.

The mission of an old path church is to preach this gospel message (see above) to every person in the world, in every generation (⁴⁹Mark 15:16). But we must follow Jesus' instructions. He told us to preach repentance and remission of sins (⁵⁰Luke 24:46-47) – not repentance only, or remission only. Here is the reason that 72% of Americans claim to be born-again Christians while the murder of the unborn continues in legalized abortion, and we continue exalting the vile homosexual lifestyle; here is the reason

46. Revelation 1:5 "Unto him that loved us, and washed us from our sins in his own blood.

47. 1Peter 1:23 "Being born again, ... by the Word of God,

48. Galatians 4:6 "And because ye are sons, God hath sent forth the Spirit of his Son into your hearts, crying, Abba, Father.

49. Mark 16:15 "And he said unto them, Go ye into all the world, and preach the gospel to every creature.

50. Luke 24:46,47 And said unto them, that repentance and remission of sins should be preached in his name among all nations.

more and more of our young people are turning to witchcraft for spiritual enlightenment, and why, as a nation, we are on a collision course with the wrath of God.

51. II Corinthians 4:4 In whom the god of this world hath blinded the minds of them which believe not ....

God's enemy, Satan, who blinds the minds of the lost so that they will not be saved (⁵¹II Corinthians 4:4), has managed to trick most churches into leaving out one or the other of these two parts of the gospel message. They either preach repentance without remission, or remission without repentance. Therefore, churches are filled with persons who cry

"Lord, Lord ..." but do not do what Jesus says ([52]Luke 6:46). The reason churches have so little influence upon the conscience of our nation is because most church members today are not truly saved. The churches must preach both repentance and remission of sins because there is no other way for men to be saved than to repent and receive Jesus for the remission (payment) of their sins. Therefore, please listen very carefully to the truth about repentance and remission of sins.

52. Luke 6:46 "And why call ye me, Lord, Lord, and do not the things which I say?

Repentance is God's command to all men everywhere to turn from sin and flee to Him for salvation from His judgment ([53]Acts 17:30; [54]26:17-18). The word *remission* means payment. The wages of sin is death, and so to preach remission is to declare that God has received the death of His own Son as payment in full for all our sins. God has commanded us to believe this truth about His Son, and to receive Him as our Lord and Savior. Therefore to preach the gospel means we declare the good news that God so loved the world that He gave His only begotten Son, that whoever believes on Him should not perish, but have everlasting life ([55]John 3:16).

53. Acts 17:30 "God now commandeth all men every where to repent.
54. Acts 26:18 "To open their eyes, and to turn them from darkness to light, and from the power of Satan unto God, that they may receive forgiveness of sins.
55. John 3:16 "For God so loved the world, that he gave his only begotten Son, that whosoever believeth in him should not perish, but have everlasting life.

What must I do to be saved?

Repent of your sins. Because you are a sinner, you have at one time or another chosen to sin against God. In the Bible, God lists the sins that are common to men ([See 56 next page]Galatians 5:19-21).

The list begins with adultery, fornication, uncleanness (physical and moral impurity), and lasciviousness (means lustful). Adultery occurs when someone who is married has sex with someone other than his, or her, spouse. Fornication is rightly understood as having sex before marriage. However, the word *fornication* (from the Greek *pornoeo*)[56] includes all sexual deviancy, such as pornography, homosexuality, incest, bestiality, and so on. Uncleanness refers to both physical and moral impurity. When one fails to use proper hygiene, he or she encourages the spread of diseases. Uncleanness also refers to moral impurity—which includes any thought or action that spreads spiritual diseases that corrupt the conscience. And lasciviousness refers to behaving in a manner that is expressive of impure sexual desires. Sexual harassment, behavior that is expressive of, or intending to arouse, inappropriate sexual interest, or enticing someone into sinful sexual behavior, are all included in the sin of *lasciviousness.*

> 56. Galatians 5:19-21
> Now the works of the flesh are manifest, which are these; adultery, **fornication**, uncleanness, lasciviousness, idolatry, witchcraft, hatred, variance, emulations, wrath, strife, seditions, heresies, envyings, murders, drunkenness, revellings, and such like: of the which I tell you they which do such things shall not inherit the kingdom of God."
>
> 57. Matthew 5:28
> Whosoever looketh on a woman to lust after her hath committed adultery with her already in his heart."

Jesus said that if we look on a woman to lust after her in our heart, we are guilty of the sin of adultery ([57]Matthew 5:28). So whether these things are done physically, or mentally, they are sinful.

The list continues with idolatry (the use of images in worship ([58]Exodus 20:4,5)), and witchcraft (communicating with the dead, Ouija Boards, astrology, horoscopes, Wicca, tarot cards, casting spells, and palm reading are all part of the sin of witchcraft). The Bible says that covetousness (lusting greedily for anything) is idolatry ([59]Colossians 3:5). And He warns us that involvement in any of these things brings us into

> 58. Exodus 20:4,5 "Thou shalt not make unto thee any graven image thou shalt not bow down thyself to them.
> 59. Colossians 3:5 and covetousness, which is idolatry.

contact with and under the influence of devils (⁶⁰I Corinthians 10:20).

60. 1Corinthians 10:20 "But I say, that the things which the Gentiles sacrifice, they sacrifice to devils, and not to God."

Then the list names hatred, variance (contentious arguing), emulations (striving to equal), wrath (outrageous anger), strife, and sedition (encouraging divisions between others). Remember that Jesus said if we hate a brother in our heart, we are guilty of murder (⁶¹I John 3:15). Who is your brother? All are born of Adam, and in that sense, all mankind are brothers. All bigotry and racial and religious discrimination, including the irrational hatred that the godless have for Christians, are sinful behaviors.

61. 1John 3:15
Whosoever hateth his brother is a murderer: and ye know that no murderer hath eternal life abiding in him.

The list goes on to name heresies (false beliefs, false teaching), envying, murders, drunkenness (use of alcohol or drugs to compromise sobriety), and reveling (partying, carousing).

In ⁶²Revelation 21:8 the Bible says that all liars will have their part in the Lake of Fire.

Remember that Adam and Eve only offended in one law of God, and they were condemned as sinners. Even if you

62. Revelation 21:8
All liars, shall have their part in the lake which burneth with fire and brimstone: which is the second death.

have offended in only one of the above sins, you are condemned by God as a sinner, and you need to be saved. God warns you that if you die in your sins, you will go into hell fire (⁶³Hebrews 9:27). But He loves you and has provided a way for you to be saved.

Even though you cannot see the Holy Spirit, He is at this very moment reproving your heart for your sins (^{See 64 next page} John 16:7-11). You should be experiencing a sense of guilt and shame, and a fear of judgment to come that you know you deserve. This is called conviction.

63. Hebrews 9:27
And as it is appointed unto men once to die, but after this the judgment.

64. John 16:7-11 "And when he is come, he will reprove the world of sin, and of righteousness, and of judgment: of sin, because they believe not on me; of righteousness, because I go to my Father, and ye see me no more; of judgment, because the prince of this world is judged.

If you are experiencing conviction, it means you are responding appropriately to the Spirit's reproof upon your heart. If you are not experiencing conviction, it means your heart is hardened in sin and that you love the darkness of lies more than the light of truth.[65] The reason you love darkness more than light is because you want to continue in your sin. You are wicked and damned to the eternal fires of hell because you love darkness more than light ([65]John 3:17-21). Even if you have established your own self-righteousness and refuse to submit to the righteousness of God, you will be judged by His righteousness and not your own ([66]Romans 10:3). Flee to God for mercy and ask Him to humble your heart and to grant you repentance before it is too late ([67]II Timothy 2:25). For those of you who are experiencing conviction, God has granted you repentance, and you would do well to receive it.

65. John 3:17-21 "He that believeth not is condemned already, because he hath not believed in the name of the only begotten Son of God. And this is the condemnation, that light is come into the world, and men loved darkness rather than light, because their deeds were evil. For every one that doeth evil hateth the light, neither cometh to the light, lest his deeds should be reproved. But he that doeth truth cometh to the light, that his deeds may be made manifest, that they are wrought in God.

66. Romans 10:3 "For they being ignorant of God's righteousness, and going about to establish their own righteousness, have not submitted themselves unto the righteousness of God.

67. II Timothy 2:25 "If God peradventure will give them repentance to the acknowledging of the truth.

God has commanded you to repent. This means you must turn from the power of Satan to God (which is to turn away from your sins to righteousness) and from darkness to light (which is to turn away from your false beliefs to the truth) and then to believe on, or trust in, Jesus Christ to save you ([68]Acts 26:18).

> 68. Acts 26:18 "To open their eyes, and to turn them from darkness to light, and from the power of Satan unto God, that they may receive forgiveness of sins, and inheritance among them which are sanctified by faith that is in me.

All who refuse to obey the gospel command to repent and believe on Jesus Christ will face the fiery wrath of Almighty God ([69]II Thessalonians 1:8; Matthew 25:41). Embrace the wonderful love of God and be born into His family and be saved today. Here is how.

> 69. II Thessalonians 1:8 "In flaming fire taking vengeance on them that know not God, and that obey not the gospel of our Lord Jesus Christ."

Receive the remission of sins. If you will obey God's command to repent and believe on Jesus Christ, here is what you need to do.

First, you must confess with your mouth the Lord Jesus ([70]Romans 10:9). This means you acknowledge the truth that Jesus Christ (means anointed King) is Lord ([71]II John 1:7).

> 70. Romans 10:9 "That if thou shalt confess with thy mouth the Lord Jesus, and shalt believe in thine heart that God hath raised him from the dead, thou shalt be saved.
>
> 71. II John 1:7 "For many deceivers are entered into the world, who confess not that Jesus Christ is come in the flesh. This is a deceiver and an antichrist.

Second, you must believe that He arose from the grave, according to the Scriptures ([72]I Corinthians 15:1-4). The Scriptures say He arose physically, that is, His body was resurrected ([73]Luke 24:39; Matthew 28:6).

Confessing He is Lord and believing He arose is necessary to be saved, but this alone does not mean you are saved ([74]Matthew 7:22; James 2:19). What next?

Third, you need to pray. The Bible says, "For whosoever shall call upon the name of the Lord, shall be saved" (Romans 10:13). To "call upon the name of the Lord" means to pray to God the Father in Jesus' Name (John 14:13). When we pray, we ask God for what we

72. 1Corinthians 15:4
And ... he rose again the third day according to the scriptures

73. Luke 24:39 "Behold my hands and my feet, that it is I myself: handle me, and see; for a spirit hath not flesh and bones, as ye see me have. (After He had risen.)

74. Matthew 7:22,23 "Many will say to me in that day, Lord, Lord, have we not prophesied in thy name? and in thy name have cast out devils? and in thy name done many wonderful works? And then will I profess unto them, I never knew you: depart from me, ye that work iniquity.

76. James 4:2 "Ye have not, because ye ask not.

want or need. To be saved, what you need is forgiveness of your sins. To receive this forgiveness, you need to ask God for it ([76]James 4:1-2).

I encourage you to find a quiet place to pray. Confess that Jesus is your Lord and ask God to forgive your sins in Jesus' name. Then thank God the Father in the Name of Jesus for saving your soul. After you have done this, according to the Scriptures, your sins are washed away, and God has birthed you to Himself by His Spirit into His family–you are now a child of God! ([77]John 1:11-13)

77. John 1:11-13 "He came unto his own, and his own received him not. But as many as received him, to them gave he power to become the sons of God, even to them that believe on his name: which were born, not of blood, nor of the will of the flesh, nor of the will of man, but of God.

78. Matthew 10:32-33
Whosoever therefore shall confess me before men, him will I confess also before my Father which is in Heaven. But whosoever shall deny me before men, him will I also deny before my Father which is in Heaven.

79. 1Peter 2:2 "As newborn babes, desire the sincere milk of the word, that ye may grow thereby

Jesus made it clear that He will deny those before the Father who refuse to confess Him before men ([78]Matthew 10:32-33). If you prayed in Jesus' name to be saved, then you need to tell someone about it. Also, as a newborn babe in Christ, you need to feed on the sincere milk of God's Word, which means you need to begin studying the Bible ([79]I Peter 2:2).

We would be thrilled to hear from you. Call the number on the presentation page at the beginning of this book and let us know you have received Jesus Christ. Allow us to rejoice with you. If you will give us your phone number, someone from the church named on the presentation page will call you and arrange to help you grow in your knowledge of the Bible.

As a Christian, you can help influence the world toward Christ by learning to be a faithful servant of Almighty God. To learn how to serve God faithfully, and make a real difference with your life in the lives of those you love, contact the church named on the presentation page of this book and join us in our effort to call America back to the old paths.

Epilogue

How to Find
an Old Path Church

THE INFORMATION PROVIDED IN this book provides what is needed to identify an old path church. Below, I have summarized seven easy to identify marks of an old path church:

1. They use the old path Bible—the Authorized or King James Bible.

2. They preach the old path gospel—not a watered down version, trimmed to the fancies of so-called seekers. And while they are centered on the work of seeking the salvation of the lost, they do not compromise either repentance or remission to win them.

3. The preaching and teaching will search the heart and expose sin (I Corinthians 14:20-21); it will emphasize doctrine, reproof, correction, and instruction in righteousness (I Timothy 3:16-17).

4. They preach an old path message that reproves the world of sin, of righteousness, and of judgment. They do not shy away from unpopular positions, and the spirit of political correctness does not control the pulpit.

5. They will worship in forms that are compatible with the holiness of God, manifesting the Spirit in obedience to the Word of God; that is, they will worship in spirit and in truth.

6. The leadership will strive to model Christ, and being Spirit-filled, to manifest Him to others; and the congregation will generally be characterized by the fruit of the Spirit.

7. And, first of all, the leadership and the congregation will place a great importance on sincere, earnest, and fervent prayer.

Pray; ask the Lord to lead you to the church He chooses for you and your family. After you have prayed, "not my will, but thine be done," then read the following verses and listen for the still small voice (I Kings 19:12) of the Chief Shepherd speaking to your heart by the Holy Spirit through the Word of God:

First, consider that the Lord's sheep are scattered:

> But when he saw the multitudes, he was moved with compassion on them, because they fainted, and were scattered abroad, as sheep having no shepherd. (Matthew 9:36)

Second, consider why they are scattered:

> For the pastors are become brutish, and have not sought the LORD: therefore they shall not prosper, and all their flocks shall be scattered. (Jeremiah 10:21)

Third, listen as He calls you to seek the old paths:

> Thus saith the LORD, Stand ye in the ways, and see, and ask for the old paths, where is the good way, and walk therein, and ye shall find rest for your souls. (Jeremiah 6:16)

Finally, consider Judah's answer: "We will not walk therein," and that the results of her refusal to heed God's call was judgment. Now it's time for you to answer, and decide the future of America.

Pastors' Reviews of
THE NEW CART CHURCH

"Pastor Scheidbach has tackled a very serious subject in The New Cart Church. Satan is alive and very active, and he has strategically infiltrated his Jezebels, along with her Baalism (the spirit of ecumenicism) into the methods of the Lord's Church. The results have been and continue to be tragic. It's time for Pastors and churches to wake up and return to the "old paths, where is the good way" and begin once again to "walk therein." Thank you Pastor Scheidbach for this timely warning and remedy."

Pastor Max H. Graves, Jr.
Liberty Baptist Church, Norwalk, CA
Professor: Pacific Baptist College, La Verne, CA

"Ecumenism is not a new attack on the work of God in the world today, and as Jerry Scheidbach ably demonstrates in his latest work, The New Cart Church, its real name is Baalism. With passion and skill Brother Scheidbach proceeds to prove that the answer for new cart compromise is the same today as it was then, and that answer is found in the old paths where is the good way. For anyone who is truly fervent about standing in the gap and reaching our generation with the pure gospel of our Lord Jesus Christ, this book is for you."

Pastor Greg Kern
Faithway Baptist Church, CA

"Pastor Jerry Scheidbach has written a book that is both compelling and informative. I highly recommend this book to any Pastor or Christian layman who desires to understand the church's contemporary problems in light of scriptural truth."

Pastor Jerry Cook
Freedom's Way Baptist Church, Santa Clarita, CA
Professor: Pacific Baptist College, La Verne, CA

"Chapter 7 of Pastor Jerry Scheidbach's new book, The New Cart Church, especially caught my attention. I agree with the author when he said, "Any church that is following the Spirit of truth will take prayer seriously. In fact they will make prayer a priority." Pastor Scheidbach shows us the revival that we need today, and moves us to pray for it. I recommend The New Cart Church to every believer interested in revival in our time."

Dr. Benny L. Beckum
Founder/President Intercessor Ministries, Inc.

"When I read this book I expected it to explain in great detail why all those attending "New Cart" churches should leave immediately and find an "old paths" church. While I was not at all disappointed, I was not expecting to be convicted over how easily I have been tempted by some "New Cart" spirits. I heartily recommend that every man who claims the call of God on his life get out his Bible and read this book.

Pastor Marshal Stevens
Calvary Baptist Church, American Canyon, CA

"The New Cart Church could have been written years ago. It is not New. But this book is timely because so many have swallowed the 'political correct' notion of 'Do Church Your Own Way'. The prologue alone should be enough to cause concern among those who 'claim' the 'Christian Explosion' is real. There is no doubt the Lord's Church will exist 'throughout all ages'. But that does not mean we should allow the deceiver free course. He should be exposed. Honest, thinking people should welcome the tenets of this book to 'dismantle it' or 'get on board.'"

Keep the FAITH
Evangelist Dave McCracken